A CTIVATING LEADERSHIP IN THE SMALL CHURCH

ACTIVATING LEADERSHIP IN THE SMALL CHURCH

CLERGY AND LAITY WORKING TOGETHER

STEVE BURT

Douglas Alan Walrath
General Editor

Judson Press® Valley Forge

ACTIVATING LEADERSHIP IN THE SMALL CHURCH

Copyright © 1988
Judson Press, Valley Forge, PA 19482-0851

Second Printing, 1989

Library of Congress Cataloging-in-Publication Data
Burt, Steve, 1949-
    Activating leadership in the small church.

    (Small church in action)
    Bibliography: p.
    1. Small churches. 2. Pastoral theology.
3. Christian leadership. I. Title. II. Series.
BV637.8.B87   1987   253   87-29763
ISBN 1-8170-1099-8

The name JUDSON PRESS is registered as a trademark in the U.S. Patent Office.
Printed in the U.S.A.

Foreword

Small churches are in a class by themselves. To overlook their uniqueness is to misunderstand them.

Unfortunately, small churches are commonly misunderstood. For example, they have long been viewed as proving grounds for new pastors. According to that assumption beginning pastors should make their mistakes in small churches; fewer people are involved and, therefore, the mistakes will be less costly. Also, those who demonstrate their ability in ministry with small churches will likely be effective pastors of larger churches.

Such viewpoints are hardly warranted. Only the most crass perspective could hold that those who are members of small churches deserve consistently lower-quality, less-experienced pastoral care than those who are members of large churches. Small churches are not smaller versions of large churches. They are qualitatively, as well as quantitatively, different. The insights pastors gain in ministry with small congregations do not transfer directly to larger congregations. In my own experience those who minister well and are happy in a small church rarely are as happy or effective when they move to a large church. Church members who are nurtured and who are effective lay leaders in small churches rarely find similar nurture or are as able to serve when small churches become larger.

Small churches deserve to be dealt with in their own right. Denominational programs in education, outreach, stewardship, etc., designed for large churches rarely suit the needs of small congregations. To draw the potential out of small congregations, those who lead them and who provide resources for them need to appreciate their potential as small churches.

This series of books is designed specifically for those who lead and support small churches. Each author is someone who cares about and understands the unique possibilities of small congregations.

I can think of no one better suited to launch a series of books about possibilities for small churches than Steve Burt. His book, *Activating Leadership in the Small Church,* is a warm and practical description of ways to identify, engage, prepare, and support both pastoral and lay leaders of small churches. As a pastor of small churches, Steve knows whereof he writes. The book is full of warm and helpful illustrations drawn from his own and other small church leaders' experiences. He offers leadership strategies and organizational approaches that work in small churches. Yet, throughout the chapters, he constantly reminds us that the small church is God's people called to be in ministry.

Douglas Alan Walrath
Strong, Maine

Contents

Introduction

In New Hampshire an elderly widower suffered a heart attack. The small church he attended heard about it and spent an afternoon together splitting and stacking his winter firewood supply.

In Maine a family lost their home in a late-night fire. They had no insurance, and they needed food, clothing, blankets, and money immediately. The first organization to respond was their local church, which delivered cases of food, boxes of clothing and blankets, and emergency cash less than twelve hours after the fire.[1]

In Vermont an elderly woman with no family needed to travel fifteen miles each way to and from the hospital to receive radiation treatments. Her local church's women's group (ten women) organized a pool of volunteers to provide transportation.

In Oklahoma a small church got intimately involved in the funeral of one of its members. More than thirty of the one hundred active members involved themselves—a dozen men designed and built a simple casket, a group of women created a memorial banner, others prepared a quilt with farewell messages, and many took part in preparing the church and speaking at the funeral service. Friends and family transported their brother in Christ to the grave site in a station wagon and filled in the grave with their own picks and shovels.[2]

What do these events have in common? First, they show people organizing themselves to care for other persons. Second, all four groups act out their caring in similar ways as the social organism we call the small church. (I purposely did not mention any denominational labels in connection with the four examples because piety and polity don't seem to matter so long as the collective caring finds expression.)

The purpose of writing this is not to foist another "small-is-beautiful" book on the buying public. Others have already offered persuasive arguments for the worth of the small church. *Activating Leadership in the Small Church* is for those already sold on it and who want to explore further and understand the dynamics small churches share—including the uniqueness of leaders in voluntary systems, the creation of favorable climates for volunteers to sprout and grow, and the importance of positive self-esteem in the face of rapid social change, inflation, and comparisons to larger churches. Rather than look at the four examples and exclaim, "How wonderful!" I would ask, "Whose idea was it? Who sensed the group's need to act? Who directed the plan of action? What was learned? How was the church's self-esteem affected? What next?" That's what this book is all about.

I cannot stress enough that this book is designed for use by both clergy and laity. I didn't write half of it for clergy and half of it for laypersons. I wrote the whole thing for all folks who hope to understand the small church and its unique leadership dynamics.

A word about the content and organization of the chapters. The first three chapters deal with the intimacy of the small church and how the pastoral leadership functions catalytically to get things done while maintaining relationships. The middle three chapters are about volunteers, church esteem, and doing what we can rather than bemoaning what we can't do. The final three chapters offer pastors and laypersons a few helpful insights and suggestions regarding times of pastoral changes.

There are a number of people in the field of small churches to whom I am indebted, particularly Douglas Walrath, Carl Dudley, David Ray, and Lyle Schaller. I've read much of their work, sat in many of their classes and workshops, and absorbed many of their anecdotes and lectures so that my mind has gotten saturated with their thoughts, theories, and stories. I've tried to give credit where credit is due, but if I've missed an acknowledgment or two, I apologize.

Thanks also go to Jerry Handspicker and Julieanne Hallman, who served on my doctoral committee at Andover Newton Theological School. Along with David Ray and Douglas Walrath, they stretched and challenged me to make a good book into a very good book.

I am also indebted to many people who have shared their small church stories and insights with me—doctoral students and student pastors, clergy and laity, Yankees from New England and Rebels from Texas, parishioners in churches I've served and church folk I've met at workshops or in small town diners. Most of all, though, I thank the parishioners who let me be a small church pastor (lover) and the hometown folks at Greenport (N.Y.) United Methodist Church who nurtured me first as an active small church layperson.

Steve Burt
White River Junction, Vermont
May 1, 1987

Barn-raisings, Baptisms, and Barbecues: The Small Church in Action

I was chatting with Henry Burroughs, the retired veterinarian in town. Henry was reminiscing about the courtship of Mary, his wife of fifty years. During World War II he had been on leave in New York City when he decided to call Mary in Vermont. The New York operator asked Henry what number he wanted, so he simply said, "Vermont. The number is Wilmington Two."

"I'm sorry, sir," the city operator replied, "But I need the *complete* number."

"That *is* complete," Henry answered. "Just Wilmington Two."

"My, that must be a small town," the operator said.

"Oh, not all that small," Henry replied. "But we are quite close-knit."

There have been many attempts to define and analyze the entity we call the small church. It often has been looked at by its numbers—number of members on the rolls, number of communicants, number of pledging units, or number of worshipers on an average Sunday. But numbers do not describe the small church any more than 3.2 describes the average American family, or any more than the number of clowns and acrobats describes the quality of a particular circus. Henry Burroughs expresses the entity of the small church as well as anyone in his statement about his small town. "Oh, not all that small," he replies to the operator who is trying to quantify Henry's town. "But we are quite close-knit," he says, describing it in relational terms. The operator is talking about a community as if it were as fixed and observable as a butterfly collection under a microscope, but Henry is speaking of a community *experientially* as a living, changing, caring entity. Likewise, to outsiders the term "small church" is quantitative and focuses on the word "small," while to insiders the term is qualitative and focuses on the word "church." It implies intimacy, unity, and relationships among people who know one another.

A friend of mine, whom I shall call Lee, found out how deceiving numbers can be. Lee left a denominational position on the East Coast so he and his family could return to their home state of Texas. He wanted to raise his family while serving a small church. Lee narrowed his final choices down to two healthy churches, each with around three hundred members and each averaging eighty to ninety people at weekly worship. Their range of activities was similar, although one church invested more time and energy in denominational issues. Having just come from a denominational post, Lee felt a slight bias toward that church, but it was still a toss-up until after the interviews.

As Lee asked questions of parishioners, the identities of both churches became clear. One church's members described their church as an active, healthy, "mid-sized church with a variety of programs." They were also aware that they were "active and influential" on the denominational level, and took pride that their choir "often performed in concert for other area churches." Their departing pastor had "taken the reins in a much larger operation" in a larger city.

The members of the second church described their church as "just a small church. We don't have a whole lot of clout with the denomination. But we're very friendly and we enjoy one another's company. We have great barbecues, and we all know one another. When there's a need, we all pull together."

Both churches were healthy and active, but the subjective data Lee gathered by interviewing the participants indicated that the first church saw itself clearly as a mid-sized church while the second saw itself as a small church—despite equal numbers. Henry Burroughs would have felt very comfortable in the second church. ("Oh, not all that small . . . but we are quite close-knit.") Lee chose the second church and has been very happy there.[1]

Since the essence of small church is subjective and experiential more than objective and measurable, I've found that the small church needs to be described by *generalizing from events* rather than by extrapolating from raw data. And because the small church is so relational, *the leadership needs to be looked at in relational terms.* Both pastors and lay leaders need to be looked at for their relational skills, not just for their management and/or professional skills.[2]

The reason I've chosen to generalize from events rather than extrapolate from data is simple. In church (and particularly in the small church), the cohesive force is not primarily theological, geographical (neighborhood), or denominational. *The primary cohesive force is shared experience.*[3] It is much like the shared experience that holds an extended family together. As years go by, new members are born into, adopted into, married into, or otherwise assimilated into the family, and a cohesiveness of shared history and experience holds it together. Stories, myths, and histories are passed on from generation to generation, and are added to by present generations. Rites of initiation and rites of passage help the binding by providing new events that allow shared experience. Each participant is drawn and held by the extended family (in this case the small church).

By looking at three types of events in the life of the small church, we can make a number of observations and generalizations. The three events I've chosen are barn-raisings, baptisms, and barbecues (caring in action, ritual, and fellowship and fund-raising—all of which are done together).

Barn-raisings

I was working on my sermon on a Saturday night when the phone rang. Fire had destroyed the home of a family in our congregation. They barely escaped with their lives. They had no fire insurance. I was too upset to finish the sermon, so I set it aside and went to visit the family, which was cramped together with relatives next door in a tiny four-room house. I prayed with them and tried to comfort them.

The next morning in worship there was an atmosphere of emptiness—almost helplessness—among the people. After the preliminaries I said, "True worship is giving ourselves to God fully, offering our *selves* as a *living* sacrifice. I want us all to go home, round up food, clothing, blankets, and money, and meet back here in an hour. We'll take the worship service to our friends."

An hour later we all piled into the little house, each carrying food or clothing. The church presented a check, and jammed together amidst the food and clothing we all sang "Blest Be the Tie That Binds."

Later someone in the congregation loaned the family a travel trailer to live in. Fund-raising events (a baked bean supper at the church and a dance at the local Grange Hall) helped produce money, and loggers donated lumber for rebuilding, which was cut by the local sawmill. A number of people volunteered time and labor through the summer months, and a new house was built. A catastrophe became a meaningful event for the community of believers.[4]

The barn-raising (or house-raising) typifies the event that can provide meaningful shared experience for the church and/or community. People work together for a cause. Such an event in the life of a church becomes part of its oral history and adds to the glue that binds the church folk to one another.

Baptisms

The most memorable baptism I ever saw didn't take place in a huge, airy cathedral with a frescoed ceiling. It took place in a drafty, small church in rural Maine, one that seated less than a hundred people and that was served by a part-time pastor whose primary occupation was school teacher. Not only that, but it wasn't an adult (believer's) baptism, nor was it done by immersion (dunking)—both of which are traditionally thought to carry a higher level of meaning. It was the sprinkling baptism of an infant done in the context of morning worship.

After the opening hymn the pastor invited all the Sunday church school children to gather around the baptismal font that he had placed in the center aisle near the front pew. Then he invited family, friends, and "anyone else who wants to see close up what's going on" to join them around the font. It was quite a picture with the Sunday church school kids, the parents holding the baby, the aunts and uncles, the cousins and grandparents, and the friends standing around the font with the pastor.

The pastor asked if the children knew what was going on. Several of them weren't sure, and there was a moment of silence. Then one of the older girls chimed in, "We're going to baptize the baby!" (Not "*You're* going to," but "*We're* going to!" That's doing theology.) The whole congregation laughed together. It was obvious that they were used to informality and that they enjoyed and encouraged spontaneity and participation.

"That's right," the pastor said. "And what will we baptize the baby with?"

The children looked at one another and shrugged their shoulders, but as the pastor lifted the cover from the font and they saw the water, several of them eagerly answered, "Water!" Everyone laughed again. "And do you think there's anything special about this water?" he asked them.

There was a long silence. It was obvious the children were thinking about it, and so were the adults. Finally one young boy dared to say, "Looks like regular water to me." The other children and the adults waited to see if the boy would be corrected by the pastor.

"That's right, Seth," said the pastor. "It's not any sort of magic water. It's just regular old tap water I took out of the kitchen faucet today. Go ahead and touch it if you like. Just plain old water." And with that the pastor dipped his fingers in it first to show the children it was all right. Then several of them dipped their fingers in.

"Ooh, it's cold," one girl exclaimed.

"It's wet," said a little boy with a lisp.

"Of course it's wet! It's water!" said another boy, and the children and the congregation all laughed together. Everyone was enjoying watching the kids discover baptism firsthand.

"We don't have special magic water for baptisms," continued the pastor, "because we don't need it. We believe God can make tap, spring, river, or pond water—*any* water for that matter—special. In that same way God can take any regular old person—or any new person like this new baby—and make them special."

The children paid rapt attention as if hearing a good bedtime story. It was clear they somehow sensed the mystery of it even with plain old water.

"When we baptize *adults* into the Christian faith," he continued, "we ask them if they'll organize their lives around Jesus Christ and his teachings. But today we're baptizing a baby, and a baby can't answer that question yet. Maybe later. So today we're asking the baby's parents, and relatives, and all these friends here if they'll help raise this baby according to *their* belief in Jesus. But it's still *the baby* we're baptizing, isn't it?"

The children nodded yes.

"In some ways baptizing a baby is like your mother giving you a kiss on the forehead on your first day of kindergarten.

It's not magic, but somehow we believe there's something powerful, special, and protecting about that nice wet kiss on the forehead, don't we? It's a seal of love to guard us and to get us to school and home again safely. A baby's baptism is something like that—like the kiss of Jesus—to guard and to guide that baby until he or she is old enough to decide to follow Jesus on his or her own."

After that the pastor took the baby in his arms and proceeded through the more formal parts of the ritual, including dipping his fingers in the water three times and making the sign of the cross on the baby's forehead three times, saying, "In the name of the Father (first cross on the forehead), and of the Son (second cross), and of the Holy Spirit (third), I baptize you into the Christian faith."

Then all the kids started clapping as if they had witnessed a new birth, and all the adults joined in! The pastor carried the congregation's newest Christian up the center aisle and back to show her off. Before the parents sat down, though, the president of the women's group presented a Dutch Cradle Cross for the baby, and she and the pastor shook hands with the parents and grandparents. The morning service continued, and afterward everyone gathered in the vestry for cake, coffee, and chatter. A baptism, like a barn-raising, provides another shared experience for the community of believers, both adults and children.

Barbecues

It was a warm Saturday evening in July. The narrow main street in a rural Maine town was lined with cars and pickup trucks. People were dressed in everything from coveralls to shorts and swimsuits, and were sitting on blankets or at picnic tables on the church and parsonage lawns. Families stood in line clutching paper plates and plastic utensils as they inched closer to the sweating cooks standing over the shimmering, hot charcoal pits. The prize: a barbecued half-chicken (occasionally a half-barbecued chicken) that they would surround with baked beans, potato salad, cole slaw, rolls, and a cool gelatin salad. Afterwards the diners had a choice of watermelon or homemade vanilla or strawberry ice cream. And all for only four dollars per adult, two dollars under twelve, and preschoolers free! Church members, friends of the church from the local community, and visitors could all feed their families for a cheap night out while enjoying the picnic atmosphere of a night with friends—all while feeling good about supporting the church.

A dozen men took turns tending the fires in the charcoal pits they had spent weeks readying. Dozens of women and teenagers kept the salad tables stocked while others handed out soft drinks and coffee. Still others collected trash or directed people to the bathrooms. Several of the elderly matriarchs of the church sat at a card table with the cash box, selling tickets and making conversation. Four or five teenage girls were trying to organize a free nursery and baby-sitting service in the Sunday church school rooms and nursery. Two volunteer firemen directed traffic in front of the church. A sign on the telephone pole and another on a wooden sandwich board proclaimed NINTH ANNUAL CHICKEN BAR-B-Q. An important event in the life of this small church was going on, and it required the efforts and cooperation of many. The barbecue provided the shared experience of working together—part of the glue that holds a small church together.

The Small Church in Action

Barn-raisings, baptisms, and barbecues aren't the only events in the life of a small church, but they are certainly representative of its scope of activities. Both pastors and lay leaders will find leading the small church easier if they understand some of the dynamics involved.

First, the members of the small church often act *en masse* rather than in the many small sub-groups that typify mid-sized and large churches. Carl Dudley compares the small church to a "single cell," like a paramecium that assumes all the functions of ingestion, locomotion, reproduction, and so forth, in one cell. But Dudley believes the small church is also a single cell of caring.[5] In the small church the majority of people attend and support *most* of their church's functions—even if the function isn't that member's particular cup of tea. Everyone feels needed, wanted, and valuable in the small church.[6] It is safe to say that if the barn-raising, the baptism, and the barbecue had been events in the life of the same small church, eighty percent of the participants would have been the same people.

Second, the small church is intergenerational in its work, play, and education.[7] Whether it is by chance, choice, or necessity, the small church's calendar is dominated by events involving children, parents, grandparents, and sometimes great-grandparents (or unrelated people who fill the various roles). The baptism was a classic example of the joy of intergenerational interaction around a sacrament. At the chicken barbecue generations worked together, ate together, and learned from one another; values were transmitted from generation to generation as service to the church was modeled. The barn-raising and its subsequent activities demonstrated generations working together in outreach.

Third, and following closely on the heels of the second, Christian education in the small church depends less on the classroom and more on overall church life. Christian education is integrated into the fabric of the small church's entire life together.[8] *Transmitting values is of higher priority in the small church than transmitting information,* and that is accomplished by participation, by intergenerational modeling, and by hands-on experience. The methodology is primarily *inductive* rather than *deductive.* During the baptism, even when the pastor taught about baptism didactically, he allowed room for people to draw their own conclusions when he used the analogy of the kiss on the forehead. That's not doctrine or dogma, but it gets the *idea* across in understandable terms—not unlike Jesus comparing the kingdom to a mustard seed (Matthew 13:31).

In the ongoing life of the church itself values are transmitted by *implicit* messages as well as explicit teachings. "Service to the church is important," said the barbecue. "Helping those in need is important," said the barn-raising. "Baptism is important. My participation in the life of the church is important." Messages and values everywhere.

A young woman in a New Hampshire church told me how she learned to be a Sunday church school teacher:

> "I don't recall a lot of what Miss Sage taught us on paper, but I sure remember the way she held me on her lap during Sunday church school. My parents didn't do that much. They weren't real physical. Miss Sage taught me what a great feeling it was to be held and hugged—even by someone who wasn't your own mother. She taught me how to be an affectionate mother and Sunday church school teacher, so even when I'm with kids who aren't my own, I hold them and hug them just like Miss Sage did with me. *It's a value, I guess.*"

Small churches are good at transmitting values.

Fourth, the small church values informality and spontaneity in its members and leaders. A big premium is placed on allowing persons to be persons so they may develop to the full potential God has in mind for each. At the baptism the remarks, giggling, and questions of the children were encouraged by the pastor and applauded by the congregation. Everyone shared in the joy of the children's discoveries. Informality allowed room to be "real."

Fifth, the small church places a high value on fellowship, intimacy, and meeting relational needs.[9] Meals seem to dominate the social calendar of small churches just as they did during Jesus' ministry. The coffee and cake after the baptism, the chicken barbecue, the baked bean supper to help raise money for the barn-raising—all provide relationship building time, time for people to get to know and love one another. Such times can be very sacramental, serving as informal Communion time when members and friends exchange information, provide care and healing for one another, and plan and exchange ideas for ministry.

Sixth, shared events are a way the small church includes new people. Inclusion in the local church is partially dependent on official membership, but it is more dependent on partaking in the bread of shared history and the cup of experience, the binding force of the church community. Those who worked on the NINTH ANNUAL CHICKEN BAR-B-Q have a stake (not a steak) in that church. Those who participated in the first through the ninth barbecues really have a stake in it! Likewise, those who took part in the caravan of food and clothing after the house fire have been incorporated by an emotional and spiritual tie into that church. Now they have a language of experience to speak with. And so too, those who were part of the baptism have been knitted into the very life fabric of that small church—even if they were attending for the first time, because they now become "the Wrights, who started attending the week little Donna Ducharme was baptized." Being incorporated into the memory, history, and events of the church is a way of becoming part of the small church.

Seventh, the small church has a high people priority.[10] The president of the women's group, by presenting the Dutch Cradle Cross, helped make the baptism a special occasion for the parents and baby by giving something especially for *that* child. The pastor also showed a people priority by taking time to include the children rather than just getting to the more "official" parts of the ritual. And the church made sure it allowed for plenty of "people time" after the worship and baptism.

The barn-raising demonstrated an obvious people priority, too. But making people a priority over program is another facet of "people first" in which the small church excels.[11] A pastor in a small western Massachusetts church fondly referred to his church's choir of three as "one flat, one sharp, and one undecided." Yet every week he and the members of the congregation would honestly thank their choir and tell them what a nice job they had done. They weren't being dishonest. They were saying they recognized and appreciated their efforts.

In a coastal Maine community where I preached several times, the organist was ninety-two years old and had grown quite deaf. She was touted as the oldest active church organist in the state, and you could immediately sense she was proud of that identity. During my pastoral prayer I must have made some sort of ambiguous gesture, because she began to play the *Gloria Patri* while I was still speaking. People were on their feet in a flash, singing the *Gloria* and chuckling quietly at my plight. Later, when I announced Hymn 84, she started playing a different hymn and everyone had to play "Name That Tune" until they could figure out a little of it, look it up in the index, and turn to the new hymn. But the congregation did it with graciousness, good humor, and patience just as they had done for week after week. They were blessed with a strong sense of people priority.

Eighth, the small church relies heavily on its laity.[12] Lay volunteers serve on committees, organize pledge drives and fundraisers, staff the choir and church school, and do much of the informal visitation. Usually the organist, the custodian, and the choir directors are the only paid persons besides the pastor (more frequently as churches approach midsize). More and more churches now are hiring part-time secretaries to lighten the pastor's administrative load, allowing her or him to spend more time in relationship building. Often though, all the positions other than pastor are filled by volunteers. Working with a volunteer staff is much different from working with a paid staff (as in a large church) where the accountability structure tends to be more "enforceable."[13]

Ninth, the small church relies heavily on laity *to provide leadership*—not just to supply workers to accomplish tasks. One-fourth of all Protestant congregations in North America report less than thirty-five persons at their principal weekly worship service, and one-half report less than seventy five.[14] Staffing for those small churches is often done by hiring part-time clergy or seminarians, by sharing pastors with other churches, by hiring bivocational pastors, or by training certain laypeople to perform pastoral duties such as worship leadership. With clergy time at a premium, laity in small churches provide much-needed leadership.

But laity don't only provide leadership due to the absence of clergy. Laypersons often are better qualified than clergy (especially those who are newcomers to the area or to the profession). Laypersons usually know the parish needs better—especially in the case of commuting clergy. And laypersons often are more attuned to the resources available to meet local needs. The pastor of five small churches in northern New Hampshire told me, "During the morning announcements at each church on my circuit, I find out what ministries and special events are under way or in the planning stages. It's so different from the large church where I was an associate pastor during seminary. Back then I thought *the minister* called the shots and announced what ministries the church would engage in."

Tenth, small churches need good small church pastors, women and men who can provide leadership rather than management, who can build up the laity and inspire them so they trust themselves to make decisions and follow through on them rather than to simply hear decisions and carry out orders. David Ray writes:

> "What is not needed in a small church is an executive director, expert, or boss. What is needed is a hybrid of a catalyst, juggler, priest and prophet, cheerleader, Ann Landers, traffic cop, best friend, janitor, and a bit of P.T. Barnum."[15]

The good small church pastor is usually part of the community, part of the extended church family, and as such is valued more *for the person he or she is* than for the skills he or she possesses. The part-timer who officiated at the baptism was important in the service more for who he was to the family and congregation than for what his qualifications were. He was part of the community in such a way that his personality, his spirituality, his parable of the kiss, and even his touch enhanced the level of meaning for the participants. The power of his wet fingers in the parents' minds was not very different from the power of Jesus' hem for the woman who touched his garment in a crowd (Matthew 9:20).

Small church folk want a pastor who will share not only in the mysteries of the faith, but also in the scratching of heads over the mysteries of life. They want someone not to stand *over* them, but to stand *beside* them—beside them washing dishes at a church supper, beside them in a court case or social security hearing, or beside them in a graveyard unable to make sense of a suicide or a hit-and-run death. They want "a real person" they can know "like a member of the family," not a "cardboard professional." They want someone who is real and close, not detached and distant, "to say the words over Uncle Henry" or to solemnize the marriage of Mary Beth and Jim "who both grew up in our church and went through our Sunday church school and youth group." They want someone they know and love to gather the saints together "when it's time to get little Barbara baptized."[16] The small church needs pastors who are close and intimate and "real."

2

"Our Pastor's So . . . Real": Small Church Pastors

While she was preaching old Mr. Harner's funeral sermon—right smack in the middle of it—she began to cry. And we all began to cry along with her. She cares so deeply for her people!"

One Sunday morning during the prayer concerns, we heard a high-pitched sound like one of those new watches that goes off on the hour. So Jim, our pastor, stopped what he was doing and told us to take two or three minutes to say hello to one another in the pews. Meanwhile he went over to Minnie Patterson's pew—she's eighty-nine this summer— and he helped her adjust her hearing aid, which had been the source of the screeching. I wish you could have seen him bending over Minnie there, putting it back in her ear. Her not hearing what Jim was saying, and Jim not knowing a thing about hearing aids. Looked like a Norman Rockwell magazine cover. But that's the way Jim is. He's our pastor.

Such comments are not unusual in small churches. They express the intimate nature of the relationship small churches and their pastors have. Carl Dudley hits the nail on the head when he declares that small churches want a "lover" for a pastor, "one who will call them by name, who walks with them through the uncertainties and transitions of life."[1] Such comments also suggest that the nature of pastoral authority is less dependent on office or title than on the identity of the pastor in relationship to the members of the small church family.

The comments also show that small churches crave pastors with a strong people orientation before a strong program orientation. *Good small church pastors tend to be people-first in their theology.* Rules, regulations, church dogma—even the movement through the morning worship service—take a back seat to people's needs, as with Minnie and her hearing aid.

It's that theology that Jesus spins out when he is questioned about the legality of his disciples picking grain on the sabbath (Mark 2:23ff). He suggests that the intent of the Law is to give a day of rest *to benefit people*—not to demand a slavish adherence that serves only to oppress the oppressed even more. "The Sabbath was made for humankind, not humankind for the Sabbath."

One small church pastor in the western mountains of Maine was asked to conduct a funeral for "Fudge," the pet hamster of a ten-year-old girl. Not only did the pastor conduct the funeral (one older parishioner who had transferred in from a large urban church thought it *might* have been a sacrilege!), but he used the opportunity to talk to the Sunday church school children about death, dying, and grief. The story of "Fudge's funeral," now near-legend in that community, still circulates around town when people talk about *caring* pastors.

Good small church pastors tend to be "in culture."[2] That's not the same as saying they *have* culture. Some do; some don't. In the world's eyes many flunk the test, but so did the carpenter from Nazareth who roamed the countryside on a shoestring supping with sinners, prostitutes, and tax collectors. While Jesus may not have *had* much culture in the world's eyes, he was certainly "in culture." When he preached to farmers, he used agricultural words and images like harvest, sowing seeds, reaping, and burning chaff. In fishing towns he spoke of casting nets and fishing. The hearers got his point because

Jesus was "in culture." He was an insider. He knew the inside jokes. He knew the history and tradition of the area. Jesus was "in culture."

At a community Good Friday service in central Vermont, I heard a fifty-five-year-old part-time pastor (full-time dairy farmer) preach on Christ's Fifth Word from the Cross: "I thirst." It was a cold winter night in that farming community, and most of the people had only experienced a desert through movie-going. But that pastor created a vivid image of extreme thirst by describing putting hay into a barn loft at the end of a hot summer work day. We were all with him under a tin roof with the air thickly swollen with hay dust, and we *knew* how Jesus must have felt on a cross in the hot sun. We couldn't wait for the service to end so we could enjoy the refreshments the women's group had prepared! Describing a desert with hot sand and a dozen camels would not have been nearly as effective as the "in culture" illustration by this "in culture" pastor.

Being in culture also means having the savvy to know that a high value is placed on the small church pastor preaching the high school baccalaureate service or the town square Memorial Day service in conjunction with the American Legion, the VFW, and the Disabled American Veterans. And it means acknowledging the presence and efforts of the local Boy Scout troop and its leaders at a worship service every February—even though their main purpose in attending is to earn merit badges rather than to worship—and even though none of them or their leaders ever joined or attend the church. A good small church pastor may also learn to be in culture by observing and listening to what is important and of value to those in the community he or she serves. This means not waging a one-person war against tradition, but looking hard instead to see the values and reasons that spawned such events. A large part of the pastor's authority depends on taking seriously the individual's or the community's customs, values, and culture.

Good small church pastors tend to be characters as well as to have character.[3] Small churches make pastors characters in their ongoing drama of life—if they love them. In larger churches there is a tendency to apply the word "character" as an attribute. "Our minister *has* character." But small churches use it to describe the delight and depth of a loving relationship. "Our pastor's really a character! Know what he/she did last week?" To be a character in a small church's life is to be made real. To be part of a people's history and folklore (not just in the statistics column)—that's like the Velveteen Rabbit discovering that to be made real is to be hugged and used and loved until one's whiskers wear off and one gets loose in the joints![4]

It's not uncommon to hear tales of a small church pastor who has become a character in the town's history. "Remember Pastor Wiswell? How about the time he stood too close to the grave—and he fell in, pulling all those flowers in on top of himself! Now there was a pastor who wasn't afraid to pull some boners like the rest of us do!"

Good small church pastors tend to be patient, realizing that the small church operates on a different time system from the rest of the world.[5] Its time is distinctly its own, for its existence and essence (shared experience) are largely independent of the outside world. (That may account for the many charges that small churches are too parochial or too local-minded.) But the patient small church pastor sees that the small church has survived and ministered, and will survive and minister, long after its pastors have transferred their membership to the Larger Parish above.

Small church time is relational, not linear, and small church folk operate on "people time" (as Pastor Jim showed with Minnie Patterson and her hearing aid).[6] The people are less likely to fidget when the clock strikes ten and worship hasn't begun—especially if they can take a head count and see that Minnie Patterson hasn't arrived yet. After all, they didn't choose to attend a small church worship service so they could watch the clock. They came to enjoy being together with one another in the presence of God. If Minnie (a retired truant officer, by the way) hasn't arrived by 10:03 or 10:04, Mr. Lockwood, the retired principal, will duck out to check on her while Pastor Jim simply begins a bit late. (Nothing like a tardy truant officer!) If Minnie doesn't come in with Mr. Lockwood by the time of prayer concerns, she'll be mentioned by name and prayed for.

One frustrated young pastor, still mastering the art of pastoral patience in his small church, expressed his dismay this way: "Our annual meeting is two hours of small talk, chit-chat, and outright gossip followed by five minutes at the end of the meeting when we vote to do it the same way we did it last year!"[7] He needed to learn that the *business* was not necessarily the *purpose* for gathering, but that renewing social ties, comparing health information, and keeping relationships alive were an annual expectation held by those who attended the "business" meeting. They were attending to the business of life!

Good small church pastors tend to gain authority by sharing the power or giving it away. To give away power is to *em*power! It is the pastor's way of saying to the laity: "I trust you, and I believe in your ability to make decisions and carry them out." The power in the small church doesn't automatically come with the office, with the title, or the special clothing. It is an authority bestowed on the pastor by those he or she serves— based on the relationship that is developed. While a larger church may work more like a business (with management and workers in a definite pecking order), the small church is more like a marriage or a family. It is more covenantal than contractual.

One of the first questions I face when moving into a new pastorate is "How often do you want to serve Communion?" It seems like a simple and straightforward question, but it is also a probing question that asks: "How much power are you willing to share with us? Are you a tyrant?"

If I say "Once a month," I have done nothing to enhance our relationship as pastor and parish right from the start. Sometimes the asker will say, "The last pastor did it every other month." That statement can sometimes point to underlying feelings of powerlessness among the laity. At its gloomiest the statement means, "Will your demands be the same as or different from our last monarch?"

My response is to say, "Why don't we keep it the same as it has been, at least until the church board can talk it over afresh and decide?" The message is clear then that I intend to share and empower. If that is the message I send, I need to be consistent in later matters, too, so the trust will continue to build and laypersons will keep risking.

The small church pastor who can resist the temptation to make the quick, easy decision, who can resist the temptation to *control* the decision, who is secure enough to share or give away the power of decision (without avoiding responsibility), *will not lose power but will gain authority in the eyes of those who have been empowered.*

The pastor in a small church in western Massachusetts was at a church council meeting. The regular schedule for Communion meant the church celebrated the sacrament on the first Sunday of every month. But this year Easter fell on the first Sunday in April. A woman raised the question of whether the pastor still intended to serve Communion on Easter Sunday when there would be a full church, several baptisms, and three extra pieces of music in addition to two choir pieces.

The pastor answered, "Why wouldn't we have Communion? It's the first Sunday of the month, and Easter is as appropriate a time as any for serving the Lord's Supper."

The woman continued, "But people will have had the chance for Holy Week Communion at the Maundy Thursday service only a couple of days before. And there will be a lot of people who come to church only on Christmas and Easter. Plenty of them will feel uncomfortable if they haven't taken Communion for a while. And the service will run an hour longer than usual if we add it to all the other extra stuff Easter Sunday. I just think a lot of them won't come if they hear we're having Communion."

The pastor, feeling he was in a win/lose situation, finally "exerted pastoral authority" and barked, "We'll have Communion on Easter Sunday."

The woman didn't sense the finality and asked, "But why?" The pastor retorted, "Because I'm the pastor, and the conduct of worship is my area. We'll have it."

That ended the discussion. That ended the communication. The woman and her family were not in their home church on Easter Sunday.

What would have happened if the pastor had turned to the gathered church council (which until then only could look on helplessly during this war) and asked, "Well, what should we do?" That would be *empowerment*—giving the council the power to talk it out and arrive at a responsible decision that best served the church.

What did the pastor gain by "pulling rank"? Certainly not power. And certainly not pastoral authority—at least not in the life of that woman. *Pastoral authority is the opportunity and permission to act in a person's life in God's name—and that authority has to be given by the woman herself.* What chance does the pastor have to gain it now? And consider how much authority would have been gained by allowing the church council to act—*no matter what their decision was—even if it wasn't the decision the pastor wanted made.* Empowering the laity by giving away or sharing power is one of the greatest gifts a pastor can bring to the small church. Authority in the small church is never something *demanded;* it is always something *given.* But beware the consequences of empowerment: lay leadership will develop and activate the small church!

Lastly, *good small church pastors tend to believe in humankind's basic goodness rather than its basic depravity.* [8] The best small church pastors spend much time telling and showing their people they trust them, telling and showing them how good they are, telling and showing them they're appreciated. They do lots of pulpit acknowledgment, plenty of back-patting, and much visible and ceremonial handshaking. Some of them even present certificates to the lady who arranges the altar flowers, to the man who hauls the parsonage trash to the dump, and to the young lad who shovels the snow from the church door in winter before morning worship. Such pastors act out their belief in the goodness of people by touching them, by talking to them, and by thanking them. Those small church pastors who are most loved, who are most often given authority to touch people's lives, seem to believe that God has given them a certain flock of people, not to badger, bother, or browbeat, but to love and appreciate— warts and all.

3

Relational, Inspirational, Transformational: How Good Small Church Pastoral Leadership Sets Lay Leadership in Motion

The Friendly Ridge Community Church had been served by seven different student pastors over a nine-year stretch. But when a faithful member left the church a modest endowment in his will, the church decided to call its first full-time pastor in over a decade. After six months of interviews, the church called the Rev. Robert Boss as their pastor. Rev. Boss was thirty-three, married with two boys, and had entered the ministry later in life than some (he began seminary at thirty) after a fairly successful career in business management. He possessed organizational and management skills, business experience, and he had an excellent speaking voice. He was energetic and had a record of efficiency backed up by many certificates attesting to his branch of the business having met and exceeded its production goals. The church was looking for "a strong leader," and Boss was the perfect choice.

"The Boss," as people came to refer to him, was asked to leave after a year. Attendance at worship was halved by the time he finally drove his moving van away from the parsonage fifteen months after he preached his first sermon at Friendly Ridge.

What happened at Friendly Ridge? How could such a perfect match turn out to be such a perfect mismatch? I asked a few questions of the church folk after The Boss left.

"*His* ideas were the only ideas that counted. He'd ask for our suggestions, but when we offered some, he didn't take any of them seriously. It was just for show."

"He thought he was a general, telling everyone what to do. That's why we called him 'The Boss.' But it really wasn't funny."

"He told us we weren't allowed to sing Christmas carols until after Christmas, and then it would only be until early January and Epiphany. We always used Christmas carols to get us into the spirit during Advent."

"Our one-hour worship services started lasting an hour-and-a-half; and then it was two hours. He just went on and on, telling us how sinful we were and how poorly we supported overseas missions. I guess he didn't appreciate the fact that we dug a lot deeper than we thought we could afford just so we could add to the endowment and hire him full-time. It was a real pinch to keep him, but when he took *that* attitude, nobody much cared to keep him!"

"I always felt like he was *using* us. He had goals and we were means to his end."

"He kept trying to make us feel guilty about having a steeple fund to replace the rotting steeple. [He had] no idea how we *felt* about a steeple."

To try to organize and run a small church like an army or a business is unfair. It is counterproductive and threatens the very *raison d'etre* of the small church where *being* is primary and *doing* is secondary. ("Smaller churches are not known by what they do but by who they are.")[1] Armies with their squads and batallions, and businesses with their flow charts and chains of command, *do not function around a primary goal of enhancing their participant's relationships.* (What is unique about the church—and particularly the small church—is that the maintenance of relationships is both a means and an end; we are called to love one another, but in so doing we are energized and motivated by a sense of mission to reach beyond ourselves). Armies and businesses work toward accomplishing a goal, capturing a target, or attaining a sales quota, and people—no matter how good the employee benefit plans or the respect levels, are still secondary to the accomplishment or the goal or objective. The Boss, with his business management skills and product orientation, found that the small church didn't respond to a whip-cracker "lording it over" them. As The Boss perceived people's failure to respond to his leadership, he began using guilt and negative reinforcement as motivators. His insensitivity to people's areas of pride (struggling to pay a full-time pastor) and his failure to comprehend and value their symbols (their steeple represented their return to full-time ministry) were his undoing. The Boss also violated the small church's sense of *who it was* by trying to "make them over" (changing the length of worship; not allowing carols in Advent). Further, since Friendly Ridge had been served in recent years by short-stay student pastors, the church had learned to rely on its lay leadership. But The Boss came in and took charge single-handedly, sending the laity a clear message that they were no longer vital to the church's life and ministry (at least not as decision makers). He also declared that *doing* and *keeping up* (with the bigger churches regarding mission giving) were the new watchwords. Friendly Ridge, which had always depended on "friendship evangelism" or an "attraction model" to draw new members in, was told it would have to begin *training* home visitors ("a sales force," one woman said).[2] Is it any wonder The Boss never became "Pastor Bob"?

Chapter 2 suggested general characteristics of good small church pastors. With the introduction of the ninth item, however—gaining authority by sharing power—the critical issue of *leadership* emerges. The Boss failed to gain *authority* in people's lives (though he had a sense of *power*). The people never invested him with the name "pastor," which was for them a relational term describing respect, mutuality, and empowerment through shared decision making.

A closer look at the small church model can help leaders

better comprehend the small church. Rather than the military or business model, we need to compare it to the extended family.[3] It works better because it is relational. For example, the fact that eleven-year-old Clara Billings sings at the annual Billings family reunion is more important than the quality of her performance. Likewise, in a small church the three-voice choir is appreciated more for its efforts than for its product. (The Boss, after hearing the choir, might have announced that the choir needed more voices and that the organist would screen volunteers after worship.)

Members of an extended family find their reason for being together is *being together* (emphasis on either word or both). At times they seek to accomplish goals—like producing a family cookbook or a book of genealogy. But even with the cookbook, though some sales are to outsiders, the main reason for doing it is to collect *the family's* recipes (which represent the family itself). Like the members of an extended family, some members of the small church family are together much of the time, others some of the time, and others annually or less often. Some may work together, go fishing together, or vacation together. Members are of various ages and gather for rites of passage such as weddings, funerals, baptisms, promotions, and graduations (including school, church school, and confirmation). Lifestyles and values may vary, and belief systems become modified by relationships both inside and outside the family. Small churches, like extended families, may gather simply to *be* the small church family. During those times they transmit values, share their history, and deepen their particular culture.

The comparison of the small church to the extended family is important in understanding leadership, too. Extended families don't really run under management (maybe The Boss did). Instead, people seem to assume *leadership roles.*

Take the Newton-Lewis clan's barbecue, for example. Aunt Elvira organizes the barbecue and asks Cousin Jemima to take care of the invitations. Six months before the scheduled reunion, the Lewis part of the Newton-Lewis clan gathers for Thanksgiving dinner at Uncle Freddy's and several reunion dates are picked. Cousin Jimmy's wife, Linda, will make three phone calls to touch base with other branches of the clan to finalize the best date. Somehow all the planning will get done and the barbecue pits, volleyball net, and horseshoe pits will be in place in time. Grampa Lewis will preside, although his brother J.J. will tell most of the family stories because he's the storyteller. There will be traditional leadership roles like storyteller; short-term leadership roles like fourteen-year-old Barry getting the younger kids to help set up the tables; and specialized leadership roles like Reba showing the twins, Melba and Myra Newton, how to help Granny Nugent out of the van since her stroke left her partially paralyzed. Royal Lewis will serve as toastmaster again, and Lefty Lewis, who lost his hand in the war, will tend the fires and cook, showing the younger nieces and nephews how to do it. If you ask whose idea it was, someone will probably say, "Oh, it was Nan's. *We all wanted to do it, but she got us rolling.*" *Leadership* everywhere. Short-term, long-term, traditional, volunteer, volunteered, in-training. Lots of role-filling and role-modeling. And yet in all that there is one person assuming a role like that often filled by the small church pastor. Nan. Nan is clearly identified as *the* leader (the spiritual leader?), the only one who sensed the extended family's needs and who motivated them to satisfy those needs. Nan didn't suggest a reunion in the form of a barbecue to meet *her* needs. As the *leader* she sensed *the family's* needs, *made them her own,* and began to marshal everyone's energies and resources toward satisfying *the common need.*

James MacGregor Burns, in his book *Leadership,* writes that

leadership over human beings is exercised when persons with certain motives and purposes mobilize, in competition or conflict with others, institutional, political, psychological and other resources so as to arouse, engage and satisfy the motives *of the followers*[4] (Italics mine).

That's Nan! She wasn't hired for the leader's role, nor was she elected. There was no title, and it wasn't a formal position. But no matter who was grand marshal or toastmaster, Nan was clearly *the leader*—the one who helped the followers meet their needs (that she sensed and articulated). The contrast between The Boss' management and Nan's leadership is pointed up by Burns's statement: "Leadership, unlike naked power wielding, is thus inseparable from followers' needs and goals."[5]

Transferring Nan's example of leadership to the small church, if the pastor develops a relationship with the congregation, reads and internalizes their needs, and inspires them to mobilize and satisfy those needs, *the other needed leaders will surface to fill the variety of leadership roles that appear—because the participants will be responding to their own needs instead of the leader's needs.* But it requires developing the relationship first. David Ray suggests that what the congregation wants is "not a scholar, therapist, manager, or expert, but a member and a leader of the family."[6]

Before the pastor can inspire, though, he or she must first work at developing the relationship—not by standing *over* as The Boss did ("naked power wielding"), but by standing *beside* or *in the midst of* as Nan did (leadership). Carl Dudley says

> management skills can be learned, but leadership is discovered in relationship to a group who confirm the leader with particular authenticity. . . . The power of the pastor stems from the pastor's willingness to walk with the congregation through the abyss, through the mysteries of life.[7]

Nan's leadership came out of her relationship with the clan. In suggesting a barbecue, Nan knew that, given people's financial circumstances, travel and lodging needs, health problems, work schedules, baby-sitting needs, and abilities to contribute meaningfully in time, cash or leadership, a barbecue beat a catered banquet with a dance band. Not only was Nan patient and in culture, but she didn't feel the need to control the whole affair. She gave a clear signal that said, "I believe in the worth of our extended family, and I also trust that our people are capable of getting things together." Then she got out of their way, empowering them.

This special type of leadership, characterized by the leader helping the followers identify and meet their needs, is called transforming (or transformational) leadership by Burns. It is often described as "elevating, mobilizing, inspiring, exalting, uplifting, exhorting, evangelizing."[8] It is transformational in that "the leaders throw themselves into a relationship with followers who feel 'elevated' by it and often become more active themselves, thereby creating new cadres of leaders."[9] Remember the barbecue? Leadership everywhere!*

In Chapter 1 I mentioned our church's response to a family whose house burned. I was able to provide transformational leadership because, like the shepherd who knows his flock, I sensed my people's need to act and I knew their resources. I not only knew the needs of the homeless family, *but I also knew the needs of the church folk to act.* I offered them a way to organize and meet *their need* (and in the process to meet the needs of the family, too). Because I knew my people, I was able to *inspire* them (literally, to "put the spirit in them"). Such transformational leadership is what small churches need and seek. Douglas Alan Walrath writes:

> An increasing body of research indicates that adults in this age-group respect clergy most who can inspire. . . . That religious or, as I prefer to call it, 'spiritual effectiveness' is precisely what is basic to the church. . . . If a minister cannot inspire, does it matter what else he or she can do? And if a minister *can* inspire, everything else she or he can do matters more.[11]

---

*Transactional leadership, on the other hand, is a goods-and-services leadership that "occurs when one person takes the initiative in making contact with others for the purpose of an exchange of valued things."[10] For example, student and interim pastors often provide transactional leadership. But because theirs is a limited exchange of time and tasks for salary, it is difficult to develop an in-depth pastor/parish relationship that allows transformational leadership to emerge.

Walrath is right on! Who cares about business management skills or professional attributes if the minister can't inspire his or her people to meet *their* needs? Inspiration and leadership come from living in relationship with people, not by managing them from afar either emotionally or geographically. Good small church leadership will be relational, inspirational, and transformational—but nothing happens without the first.

4

Pearls of Great Price: Amazing Grace and Other Volunteers

Amazing Grace was on the sidelines when I came to town as the new pastor. During the 1960s she had been a whirlwind organizer, and she had been somewhat active in the 1970s. But in recent years Grace had become deactivated. Yet everywhere I went in town, people would mention her name.

"Back when Grace was in charge of the suppers we were the most active church in town."

"Grace organized the junior choir members."

"Grace led the fund-raising drive for nursery furniture, and her husband, Ken, was on the building committee for the Christian education wing in the sixties."

"Couldn't that Grace get merchants to donate merchandise to the church auction? Every year we'd use the money to pay the fire insurance. Now it's a general budget item, and we always feel strapped. I wish we could get Grace active again."

Amazing Grace was a local saint. More than that, she was an important symbol, a champion of the cause and a rallying point for the troops. Grace was one person the congregation believed could help snatch victory from the jaws of defeat. Even while she lay dormant, it was clear that Grace was an emotional leader in the congregation.

But Grace wasn't budging. When I went to see her at her house, we talked about the "good old days," the heyday of the local church. There was a sadness in her voice, but there was also a hopefulness. She was sad because she couldn't devote the energy she had once devoted. (Grace had been slowed down considerably by a disease similar to multiple sclerosis, so if she got overtired, she dragged along and became unsteady on her feet.) But it was obvious she wanted and needed to contribute in ways besides her pledge. I asked if she wouldn't like to serve in an advisory capacity, especially since she had been so active in many areas of the church over the years. She declined with the same sadness in her voice. Since I was still brand new to the parish and I didn't have a relationship firmly established with Grace yet, I felt a bit helpless and frustrated. But I sensed her need to be part of things, and I knew she was the key to unlocking the psychic energy of this parish of over 300 that now only saw twenty-five to thirty at worship. (There were no other programs—not even Sunday church school, women's group, men's group, Bible study, or any fellowship or fund-raising events.)

About a month after I arrived, it was Communion Sunday in the church. I had been to Grace's house for a second time only a few days earlier, and I really began to feel some of her frustration. I also sensed that she felt forgotten in her illness, a bit neglected of late, and perhaps taken for granted over the years. I wondered if her efforts had ever been acknowledged or if she had been treated like the goose that laid the golden egg.

When it came time to offer the invitation to come to the Communion rail, I realized that the lay leader (who normally would assist me), was absent. I knew I could easily serve the elements alone with only two dozen people, but instead I acted on a gut feeling. I said, "Before I invite you all to the rail to share in the meal our Lord has set before us, I need someone to help me serve the bread. I'd like to ask Grace Martin if she would come forward to help. It seems very appropriate and fitting that the person whose hands have served you for so many years at church suppers, whose hands have extended a welcome to so many of us so often, should serve this holy meal."

Grace came forward, a bit shy, but her face was radiant. She's never mentioned that Communion Sunday, but within a week of it she had organized a series of tea parties so that women of the church and community (later to become a women's group) could meet the new pastor. This "cottage meeting" concept (also known as killing twenty birds with one stone) enabled me to meet and talk with many more people than I could have by setting off on a one-to-one visitation program. And Grace, being an insider, knew whom to invite.

Grace also agreed to serve on the administrative council again, and it was her urging and guidance that started us on our successful Foliage Supper series. She also organized a nursery during the morning worship (with mothers taking turns volunteering), called parents and organized a junior choir, and generally reactivated the whole church. Further, when I need to know who might be right for a certain volunteer position, Grace can either suggest someone or (more often than not) ask him or her on behalf of the church. Her husband, Ken, has been reactivated now and is championing the church's handicapped access drive so the church can install a passenger elevator.

I'll never know just what it was that moved Amazing Grace. Was it my personal visits to her house? Was it my acknowledgments of her contributions as a volunteer leader over the years? Was it my visible show of asking for her help in doing the work of the church (the Communion service)? Or was it just that she was through feeling sorry for herself in the face of her illness? Maybe it was just the right time and season for her comeback. Maybe it was a combination of things. Who can say? But I felt like I found a treasure hid in a field or a pearl of great price. Amazing Grace, how do I love thee? Let me count the ways.

I hear many questions about how best to engage volunteers in the small church, especially considering the burnedover feeling of many of these exhausted servants of the Lord. The question is frequently posed by the student pastors I supervise, but I also hear it from frustrated pastors who are at loggerheads with their congregations. It usually sounds like this: "How do you _____ your volunteers?" (Choose any word from the following list and fill in the blank: identify/recruit/discover/enlist/find/empower/encourage/train/inspire/motivate/light a fire under/mobilize/whip up/energize/rouse/stir up/other.) The question is a loaded one for several reasons.

First, it sounds like a man trying to move a donkey that sat down in the middle of the road. The question can be paraphrased to say: "How do I get this donkey to go where I want him to go?" Too many pastors, in their eagerness to bring in the kingdom fast, act like donkey owners, treating their volunteers like dumb asses who refuse to move instead of treating them like the pearls of great price that they really are.

Second, the question is loaded because it suggests *management* rather than *leadership* (the small church leadership described earlier).* The predominance of action verbs in the list suggests that the pastor (feel free to substitute "colonel" or "branch manager" to uncover the military and corporate models in use again) is the one who is primarily responsible

---

*I am not trying to disparage *good* management, because I've seen it in both business and the church. But I do draw the distinction that because the church—especially the relational small church—is not primarily goal-oriented or productoriented, a unique brand of leadership, not management, is called for. The small church pastor is called to *lead* the followers by helping them meet *the group's* needs rather than to *manage* the group to meet the owner's/conference's needs.

I would also agree with Tom Peters that, of late, the word "management" may be suffering a negative connotation (rigidity, manipulation, product orientation). Peters says, " 'Management' with its attendant images—cop, referee, devil's advocate, dispassionate analyst, naysayer, pronouncer—connotes controlling and arranging and demeaning and reducing. 'Leadership' connotes unleashing energy, building, freeing, and growing."[1] The Boss was not only a poor small church leader, he was also an insensitive manager, the type who has contributed to the negative connotation of management.

for obtaining and training the proper personnel or middle management people to implement and complete a program. Consequently though, if the program doesn't grow out of the congregation's underlying purpose and needs, if it is viewed as "the pastor's baby" or "the denomination's canned package," then the people who are being asked to staff it may feel like pawns on a chess board. When pastors are faced with a shortage of volunteers, it's often not a lack of volunteers at all. It may be lack of ownership, interest, and choice. But the angry response of the stonewalled pastor may be to accuse the church of being "too parochial and nearsighted" or "out of touch with the work of the larger church, the church universal."

If the pastor is providing some sort of transformational leadership—that is, *if the program in need of volunteers is perceived by the members as a way to satisfy the needs of the leader and the followers together,* if it is in line with the church's purpose—then the responsibility for its success/mediocrity/failure will be felt by the entire body. More often than not volunteers will be where they are needed when they are needed. Sometimes they will even design creative strategies to overcome the limits of time, experience, skills, and traditional resources. Small churches, if allowed, can be very inventive and re-sourceful.

When I look back on my experience with Amazing Grace and other volunteer leaders, I observe that the verbs I use are not found either in the list or in management textbooks. They are words and phrases like: stumble on/fall over/get out of the way of/make it easy for/get surprised by/ask personally. None of those words connote control on my part. Many of them capture the feelings of surprise and joy at discovering the pearl of great price or the treasure hidden in the field. Even when we go personally to ask someone to head a committee or organize a drive, we do not know the answer until she or he gives it. Often, after we have gone to ask the person in fear and trembling, the person accepts— catching us completely by surprise! Volunteers! We stumble on them; we fall over them; we are constantly surprised by them. They are truly pearls of great price. *Volunteering is a conscious and responsible act of self-stewardship for God's sake.* Since it is a free choice and an act of responsibility by the volunteer, we who are leaders cannot manipulate people into becoming volunteers. At best we can discover them and rejoice at finding the treasure or the pearl. But practically speaking, how do we leaders go about the task of cultivating volunteers? How can we create a favorable climate in which voluntarism will be nurtured? Let me suggest ten key elements.

First, *use interest inventories.* Many churches hand them out at planning retreats or mail them once a year as part of their newsletter. They can be helpful in revealing interests and talents among active and potentially active members. (Potentially active members will often use interest inventories to flag the pastor that they want to get involved, so it's a good idea to follow up on these fast.) But leaders need to keep in mind that a five-day-a-week teacher, no matter how talented at teaching, may not feel like facing a classroom of Sunday church schoolers for a sixth day. The weakness of interest inventories is that they cannot tell us *when* it is the time or the season for a person to volunteer. Another weakness of the inventories is that they are usually filled out by confident, already active members who are the most likely to respond the quickest to the trumpet call. Potential volunteers and those who are not so self-confident may balk at filling out these forms. Nevertheless, inventories can be helpful in assessing the strengths of the active core.

Second, *be on the lookout.* As the railroad crossing signs used to advise: Stop, Look, Listen. We need to do this if we're to experience the joy of discovering the Amazing Graces around us. We need to *stop* and take seriously the input of our laity in searching for volunteer leaders. We need to *look* when they point toward those persons who are the Amazing Graces of the community,those persons who have been (or will be) invested with authority of leadership. We need to *listen* carefully, almost as detectives at times, to hear which persons are held in esteem and in local myth as emotional and spiritual leaders. The Amazing Graces we discover may never fill out an interest inventory, but we need to stop, look, and listen so we can begin developing solid relationships with them. It will be only then that we can dare ask them personally to provide volunteer leadership when it is needed.

Third, *encourage laity input into the church's program.* If the program grows out of and is consistent with the underlying purpose, if it is designed to satisfy the needs of the church body, and if the laity feel a sense of ownership and responsibility because they contributed to the planning of it, volunteer leaders will step forward.

Fourth, *encourage apprenticeships.* Children learn both skills and values by observing role models and by working along with adults. The intergenerational nature of the small church makes it a natural for this type of training. At church suppers skills (cooking, table-waiting, attentiveness, politeness) are passed on. Values such as the importance of serving, or working as a team, and of giving one's time to the church are transmitted. Similarly, teenagers who help teach Sunday church school are apprenticing. The experience, skills, and values they learn will make it easier for them to volunteer later.

Fifth, *cultivate close personal relationships.* This allows for fewer misunderstandings in case of a turndown, and it provides a solid basis for asking someone personally to assume a volunteer role.

Sixth, *don't make the pastor the only asker.* Amazing Grace, because of her many years as an insider and as a "volunteer-asker," is much better at enlisting volunteers than I am as the pastor. There are some persons whom I need to ask personally, but there are many more who have come to expect Grace to ask them. Cultivate and encourage other askers.

Seventh, *encourage small group programs that are laity-led rather*

than always pastor-centered. There is much good material that
lends itself to this. The Upper Room and Discipleship Resources in Nashville offer several excellent prayer studies
that come with a leader's guide and cassette plus participants' study guides.[2] They use a small group discussion
format. Neighborhood Bible Studies, Inc., produces some of
the best inductive Bible study materials I've seen, and their
rotating lay leadership approach reassures shier participants
while encouraging leadership development.[3] Small groups
are an excellent safe place to begin leadership risk-taking.

Eighth, *take time to explain to volunteers how their efforts fit into the
overall picture or purpose.* One Maine pastor organized "The
Holy Folders," a half-dozen elderly ladies in the congregation who gathered once a month to fold newsletters that
would be bulk-mailed to the entire membership. They enjoyed getting together, and they enjoyed feeling useful. But
they didn't really have a strong sense of "the big picture"
until the day the pastor shared part of a letter with them:

> "I cannot tell you how much our church newsletter means
> to me. I am in a nursing home almost three years now, and
> I have often felt such terrible loneliness. At times I have felt
> abandoned by family and forgotten by friends. Just hearing
> about our dear church and what my old friends are doing is
> such a comfort. It helps keep me going. I was pleased to read
> about the Holy Folders. What a wonderful idea. May God
> bless all of you who make our church's newsletter possible."

The Holy Folders continue their faithful folding to this
day because they understand the part they play in the overall ministry of their church.

Ninth, *step back.* True leaders know when to stand and
wash pots and pans at church suppers. But they also know
when to step back and trust others to get the job done. "The
captain bites his tongue until it bleeds" is a naval expression
that refers to a junior officer docking a big ship for the first
time.[4] It captures an essential quality of the transformational
leader—the ability to resist being an overbearing and over-
protective parent. Rabbi Edwin Friedman has drawn several

sharp conclusions from his observations of family and congregational leaders:

> "I assume that if the leader can define him or herself really
> well, express his or her own goals, differentiate himself out
> of the anxiety of the system ('stay loose'), and so on, it will
> affect the entire organization."[5]

That's certainly not a description of a manager. That's a
leader—one who can step back and bite his or her lip until
it bleeds! Friedman continues:

> "When people have been used to an overfunctioning type
> of leadership (the lone ranger pastor who tries to do it all
> alone), one of the major problems is in initiating the change:
> pulling back and letting things fall a little bit, so others can
> pick up more responsibility. The leader has to contain his or
> her own anxiety, because the change will take awhile."[6]

While the leader may *appear* to be defaulting, Friedman
says, it is "default while staying in touch."[7] Such a style is
difficult for many pastors to carry out because of the mothering instinct or need to protect. Many small church pastors
also find that being indispensable (doers at the center of
every activity) is a primary source of their own security and
satisfaction. A "default" style of leadership may at times
feel irresponsible and seem to go against the small church
pastor's grain. Nevertheless, stepping back while keeping in
touch is important in creating a favorable climate for volunteers.

Tenth, *make sure there is a highly visible reward and appreciation
system operating.* Hoopla and appreciation ceremonies broadcast a clear message: Volunteers Appreciated Here. A special
display of Sunday church school lessons, projects, crafts,
and drawings not only encourages the children, but it ap-
plauds the efforts of the volunteer teachers, too. Church
School Commencement Sunday should not only be a time
to give attendance pins to the children, but also should be
a time to celebrate the work of the teachers and aides. A
public word of thanks goes a long way in creating goodwill

and in providing a favorable climate for the cultivation of volunteers. (More on hoopla and appreciation in the next chapter.)

Volunteers are truly pearls and treasures that God has placed before us to discover and rejoice in. But as with pearls and treasures, volunteers are sometimes hard to find—especially in small churches where people are often stretched to the limit. Considering their scarceness and their preciousness, it is important to be sensitive and aware of the many facets of working with volunteers.

In June 1985 we swapped parsonages with another pastor and his family in Austin, Texas. During our vacation time we drove to San Antonio to see Texas' historic shrine, the Alamo. I had grown up on Disney's *Davy Crockett* series and John Wayne's *The Alamo,* so my emotions were steeped in the history and heroes of the old mission fort. It wasn't surprising that visitors were asked to remove their hats upon entering. Less than two hundred committed volunteers had held back General Santa Ana's army of 5,000 troops for two weeks! But what really knotted my throat was reading of Colonel Travis' challenge to the Alamo's defenders. He used his sword to draw a line in the dirt, asking all who would fight to the death to cross over. All but one did!

Small church folks often feel like the outnumbered Alamo volunteers—overworked, underpaid, asked to fight overwhelming odds in a no-win situation. This burned-over group may feel like they're being asked to cross Travis' line—to meet certain death (or at least exhaustion and burnout). Their dedication traps them. And it's not uncommon, when the nominating committee is asking members to fill an office for the upcoming year, to hear, "I wish you'd find someone else. Of course, if you absolutely can't find someone else, I'll do it again—but only if you can't find someone else." In other words: "I'm tired and I'm burned out from this undermanned situation, but I want you to know I'm still committed, and my church can count on me when the chips are really down." And these small church folks mean both parts of that statement. They *are* committed! And they *are* tired! When faced with a constant shortage of people in the face of a large number of possible programs, people often have to say no! But no is a word pastors (often trained to be program pushers) hate to hear. Consequently, what is actually responsible stewardship of self—"Pastor, pastor, go away; and I'll recharge for another day!"—is viewed by the pastor (who may grade his or her success by program effectiveness) as irresponsibility, lack of commitment, or lack of interest.

One man did leave the Alamo before it fell, choosing not to cross Travis' line. No one called him a coward or questioned his loyalty. No one challenged his commitment. Maybe he chose to "run away, that he might fight another day" for Texas. Maybe he had another Alamo he was previously committed to. Maybe his skills and life experience weren't what was needed there. Davy Crockett and his sharpshooters were invaluable in a shootout with Santa Ana's troops, but perhaps the man who left was a mapmaker who could help General Sam Houston later. Who can say? But whatever his reasons, the man *chose* not to stay at the Alamo.

The man who left the Alamo shows us something about volunteers. Not only are there a variety of reasons why people *do* volunteer, but there are many reasons why people *don't* volunteer. In the small church exhaustion in an undermanned setting is a reality that pastors ought to take seriously. But there are other reasons as well. Let's look at a few.

First: "I don't give a damn!" or "I just plain don't like you, Reverend!" While these folks are generally the exception rather than the rule, there are a few out there. Unfortunately, an insecure or inexperienced pastor (with a fragile pastoral ego) may take *any* turndown, regardless of the real reason, to be one of these two answers. In effect the pastor says, "People who refuse to volunteer either don't care for the church, or they've got it in for me personally!" Such an attitude, in addition to revealing pastoral insecurity, shows a product-first mentality that places getting the job done before taking people seriously. The integrity of the decision maker needs to be respected whether the answer is yes or no.

Second, there is a time and a season for everything and everyone. Monica may have bookkeeping experience, and the church treasurer's position may be vacant, but that doesn't add up to Monica volunteering to take the job. If she already runs the youth group, teaches junior high, serves on the Pastor-Parish Relations Committee and the Parsonage Committee, is active in the P.T.A., organizes the fall and spring rummage sales, and sings with the local theater group—and tries to work a regular job, be a spouse and a mother of three—maybe the time just isn't right for her to be treasurer. Maybe after the kids graduate. Maybe after retirement. Maybe if someone else takes a few of her other hats to free up some time. Monica is entitled to feel flattered to be asked, but she needn't feel obligated or guilty in refusing. *Volunteers need to feel free to say no as well as yes.* An old Vermont banjo player once told me, "You can only stretch a string so far." It's also true that strings stretched just right sound the best.

Third, people need to know what is expected of them in their "time, talents, and treasures." I've used the familiar stewardship phrase because *voluntarism is really the responsible stewardship of our human potential for God's sake.* I also believe that *nonvoluntarism may be a learned behavior* based on bad experience. Let's carry the example of the church treasurer job a bit farther.

Time. Monica might agree to fill in for a vacationing church treasurer, but she'd get a bit frazzled if the treasurer took sick and had to resign, extending Monica's time. Volunteers have a right and a need to know time frames.

Talents. If Monica takes the treasurer's job, imagine her panic when she discovers everything is computerized—and she knows nothing about computers, is deathly afraid of them, and has no time to consider a class even if the church pays for it! She's been doing ledger bookkeeping for years!

Volunteers have a right and a need to know how their talents match up with the talents required for the task.

Treasures. Imagine a classified ad in the church's newsletter or Sunday bulletin:

VOLUNTEER CHURCH TREASURER
NEEDED

Home or office computer experience helpful
or church will pay for beginner's evening
course.
See me or call me at home.
Pastor Jim 234–5678

Now try to imagine Phyllis Greenbrier's embarrassment and disappointment after she went to see Pastor Jim. She had a little office computer experience, wanted to get more involved in the church by using her skills, and felt reassured that the church would send her to evening school to get an even better grasp of computers. Too bad Pastor Jim ended the interview with "So what type of home computer do you have, Phyllis?" The church had no computer, and the last treasurer had kept all the records on her own home computer. Pastor Jim had assumed Phyllis (or any other volunteer for the position) would have a home computer. But poor Phyllis couldn't afford a floppy disk. Her lack of material treasure not only left her feeling embarrassed, but it left her with a bad taste for volunteering. Such insensitivity to a person's lack of treasure can often throw a wrench into the volunteer works.

Several years ago I pastored a small church in one of Maine's poorest counties. During that time I became aware just how strongly a lack of treasure impacts on voluntarism. The church was a mix of middle-class and poor people. At a budget meeting someone suggested that everybody needed to raise their pledges by five percent. But even that five-percent increase wouldn't float the new budget.

Someone suggested a paid baked bean supper that would

be open to the public. Everyone agreed. The poorer folks were excited about their chance to help the church financially by making the baked beans and by working the supper. Then one of the middle-class members said, "Of course, we expect everybody, including those of us who work the supper, to buy their dinners."

There was silence. Finally one of the poorer members said, "We just can't afford to buy tickets for our whole family. Not and work the dinner, too. I guess we just can't eat. We said we'd come and work, and we will, but we just won't eat." She was plainly embarrassed, and it was too bad it even got to that point. The supper went as planned, and the church decided not to charge those members who worked. But the lack of treasure almost had a disastrous impact on voluntarism. Volunteers have a right and a need to know the treasures that are required in connection with the task.

Fourth, volunteering can mean loneliness. Too often we fail to recognize this in our churches. Jesus sent his disciples out two-by-two. The arrangement provided safety, security, company, and someone to share the joys, frustrations, and burdens of ministry. There was always at least one other person around to appreciate the volunteer's efforts and sacrifice.

On Friday mornings when Asa Derrick drives his small dump truck to our church and later to the parsonage to pick up the trash, he is never without his sidekick, Henry. Asa and Henry worked together for years and eventually retired together. They still split wood together, drink coffee together, and now serve the church by picking up the trash together. Relationships like Asa and Henry's are what turn chores into chances for comradeship. I'm sure that if Asa didn't have Henry to share the task with, he'd be less likely to volunteer.

Fifth, the volunteer's task needs to be consistent and important in relation to the church's (or group's) purpose. (Purpose here refers to the focusing of individual energies to satisfy the group's common need.)

A cartoon in *Leadership* magazine shows three people sitting around a table, looking through booklets about outreach training. One man says with devilish glee: "When I was a kid I would go up to someone's porch, ring the doorbell, and run like the dickens. I still do it, except that our church calls it outreach training."[8]

We laugh because we may have had a similarly uncomfortable experience of door-to-door evangelism (on either the giving or the receiving end). Many small church folks find the task of doorbell evangelism (or "necktie-holding" as one New Jersey pastor called it) to be distasteful. But it may be that what appears to be *distaste for the task* is really *an unconnectedness of task to the group's purpose.* In fact, in many small churches an aggressive approach is inconsistent with the church's "friendship evangelism" or "attraction model" for assimilating new members.[9] If the pastor or a committee introduces a stewardship or evangelism program that is not *felt* (whether it is articulated or not) to be in keeping with the church's values and purpose, there will probably be a lack of volunteer support. A real tension can develop if the pastor is heavily invested in the program but the people view it as inconsistent. Such a conflict of values and commitments often sounds like this: "They're not committed to Christ! They just don't give a damn! They just plain don't like me." At those times pastors need to calm down and ask what the people are really saying in choosing not to volunteer.

Sixth, if people are being asked to volunteer for a program, the program needs to be interesting and appropriate both for the church and for the volunteers who are expected to run it. Another way of putting it is "people first, program second." Too often it is reversed. Pastors and lay leaders return from workshops and seminars chock full of enthusiasm and new ideas to spring on the parish. They may be enthused about a program that really caught fire in another church setting. But what happens when they return to find their home church cool to the hot new idea?

It could be there's a lack of energy and resources to commit to a new program right now. Small churches are made up of people, and people tire. Also, small churches can support just so many programs at any given time. Try again later; put it on hold.

It's often the case that a particular idea isn't suited for a particular small church. Our church's used clothing shop does very well, but the church down the road and off the beaten path, when it tried a similar venture, did almost no business at all. Does the difference in location have a significant effect on programs and ministries? How about the different socioeconomic factors?

Small churches, because of their lack of numbers, need to be especially good stewards of their human resources, and that calls for prioritizing programs and ministries. Given the time, talent, and treasures, what comes first in programming? When the church leaders return from a seminar, they are liable to have been caught up in carrying home the speaker's packaged program (which he or she enthusiastically pitched and sold), or they may be carrying home the denomination's latest "canned" program. When volunteers don't rush to staff these programs, maybe it indicates the programs are being given too high a priority—maybe even over the needs and resources of the volunteers.

Seventh, volunteers need acknowledgment, appreciation, and recognition. After all, much nonvoluntarism is a learned behavior reinforced by nonacknowledgment, nonappreciation, and nonrecognition. The best way to discourage volunteers in the small church is to never say thanks, never stoop to hoopla, fanfare, or barefaced appreciation (especially in a relational setting like a small church), and never treat volunteers with respect or courtesy, but instead take their time for granted. ("Mary, the bulletins need folding, and I'm very busy.") More about appreciation later.

Eighth, volunteers need direction, but they also need freedom. Too much or too little of either can create problems and resentment. I once went to a dentist who was overly directive. He treated everyone like a moron. In explaining the hows and whys of a long-term dental program to me, he failed to perceive that he didn't need to treat me like a kindergartner. I might have overlooked it had it stopped there, but when he sent me out to his receptionist to set up another appointment, he insisted on explaining to her over and over just how to arrange it. When I asked her how long she had been with him, she said it had been nearly a year, but that she was keeping an eye out for another position elsewhere. She was "tired of being treated like an idiot." The dentist had overdirected both of us— and we both resented being talked down to. Likewise, church volunteers aren't morons. They make decisions every day of their lives just as pastors do. So why treat them like kindergartners?

Overcontrol retards personal growth of church volunteers and discourages creativity and spontaneity in the church. Tom Peters and Robert Waterman, in their best-selling book, *In Search of Excellence: Lessons from America's Best-Run Companies,* note the importance of "skunk works"—"bands of eight or ten zealots off in the corner, often outproducing product development groups that numbered in the hundreds."[10] The most successful companies not only *allowed* their people the freedom to dream and create—they *encouraged* it! The balance between direction and freedom will vary with each volunteer, but allowing sufficient freedom to create and to share one's whole self can move churches to new heights.

One year I spoke at a national training event about the importance of laity-led inductive Bible studies. A large church pastor from a mid-Atlantic state said, "We have about ninety laity-led Bible studies connected with our church. Many have started up on their own without the pastors. How can we coordinate them?" Every church should have such problems with active laity! Why try to control them? Creativity and growth of individuals needs to

be encouraged. Too much control can be a turn-off to volunteers and to the whole church.

The flip side is this: too little direction can dampen a
volunteer's enthusiasm. Volunteer office workers need to
know where the files are kept, how to answer the phone,
where to get information, how to contact, and how to refer.
It's the uneasy pit-of-the-stomach feeling we've all had
when starting a new job. In working with volunteers we
need to remember it.

Other volunteers need ongoing supervision. In some
situations the challenges are forever changing. My church
custodian is a young man of nineteen. He easily handles
most of the cleaning tasks, but he has little experience in
building repairs and maintenance. One day I asked him if he
would mind changing the fluorescent bulb in the bathroom.
He told me he'd be glad to, but that he had never changed
a fluorescent bulb before, and he didn't know how to. He
needed a little supervision. I explained how to do it while I
made hand motions as if I were changing a bulb—but I told
him he ought to go and see if he could accomplish the task
by himself. He did. Later in the day he told me *how much he
appreciated my not showing him how to do it by doing it for him.*

"I learned something new today," he told me. He needed
a little supervision, but he didn't need overcontrol. As
Douglas Johnson has said of volunteers: "One purpose of
the church is to help them become more capable."[11]

Ninth, volunteers need to know that failure is allowable.
Some people don't want to risk the embarrassment of failing
in a leadership role. Others fear failure because it will reveal
their lack of _____ (fill in the blank with: education,
talent, money, stamina, and so forth). But failure is part of
life and part of honest relationships. People fail to keep
promises; people fail to get home in time for dinner; people
fail to overcome all odds. One way we demonstrate we are
human is by failing (at least part of the time). Maybe that's
why small church folks love to talk about the time their
pastor dropped the wedding rings under the piano. Like the

people in the skunk works of the best companies, volunteers need to be allowed to fail. If they are encouraged to try, they must be allowed the possibility of failing.

My church secretary was in her first week volunteering in our church office. She has a soft voice that she really cannot raise very much. I arrived back at the office late one Friday afternoon to find this note:

> A lady called me on the phone. She wanted to talk to the pastor. She was hard of hearing, and she kept yelling that she couldn't hear me. I tried to tell her I was speaking as loud as I could, but she got very indignant and told me off. Then she hung up. Am I fired?

Because of that note (no matter whether the last sentence was half-joking or serious) I knew I had to make it clear to my new volunteer secretary that failure was allowable. She has since become more confident and has very competently handled many difficult situations that have arisen. Volunteers need to know that failure is allowable.

Tenth, people need to be asked to volunteer. It's often as simple as that. "No one ever asked me to serve as church treasurer before." "When you asked for volunteers, pastor, I just assumed lots of others would do it." "You're the first pastor to ask me *personally* to do anything. All the rest just stood in their pulpits like roosters on a barn crowing at anyone who'd listen." Many will say no, but even then the level of individual and congregational self-esteem will be raised just in knowing they were deemed worthy to be asked. And the personal contact allows the *non* volunteer to explain what will allow him or her to be a volunteer.

There are many reasons people choose to not volunteer. But even in our undermanned small churches we are faced with the fact that *people do volunteer.* The 1984 Gallup Poll showed that twenty-eight percent of the respondents had donated time to religious work in the previous twelve months, and thirty-four percent had donated time in helping poor, disadvantaged, or needy people in the same twelve months.[12] We need to allow ourselves to be encouraged by those statistics. We needn't be sour on volunteers. Instead, we need to be sensitive to them, to see their nonvolunteering as responsible stewardship of self, and to treat them as they ought to be treated—as pearls of great price.

5

Holy Hoopla and Making Love to the Congregation: Creating a Favorable Climate for Volunteers

May 12, 1985 was Mother's Day. But the date was significant for another reason in the North Hartland and White River Junction (Vermont) United Methodist churches. Four times a year (Mother's Day, the Sunday after Labor Day, the Sunday before Thanksgiving,and the Sunday before Valentine's Day) a number of people are singled out from the congregations for recognition. Award certificates (suitable for framing) are handed out in the middle of the morning service. It is an important part of the informal (and fun) structure that characterizes these two small churches. It is the pastor's and the church's way of loving, appreciating, and thanking volunteer workers and leaders.

In North Hartland (average attendance of thirty), the first award was presented to eighty-year-old Mrs. Jessie Peoples.* It read:

This certificate presented to

JESSIE PEOPLES

PAUL'S EPISTLE AWARD

for excellence in letter-writing on

behalf of the Women's Group

*I have used people's names here. Rather than change the names to protect the innocent, I believe it is better to retain the names to acknowledge the deserving.

It was signed by the pastor and the chairperson of the administrative council in recognition of service to the church. Jessie was always the person to send out a get-well card, a sympathy card, or a congratulations card on behalf of the women's group. She never failed to add a warm personal note voicing the feelings of the entire group. With the award Jessie got a hug from the pastor and a round of applause.

In White River Junction (average attendance eighty-five) people clapped, cheered, and laughed together as the awards were presented. Joan Harris received the CHEERFUL OR-GANIST AWARD for her "adaptability and flexibility in playing hymns on request each week;" Bud Farrar got the LIBERACE AWARD for sharing his musical talents as a substitute pianist whenever Joan Harris was away on vacation; Maxine Wright picked up her first GOLDEN PLAY-PEN AWARD for organizing and coordinating the mothers who served as weekly nursery volunteers; Edith Jacobs received the GOLDEN HANDSHAKE AWARD for telephoning and lining up volunteer greeters and coffee hour hosts each week; Jane Snaith got the ORGANIST'S-AWAY-THE-PIANIST-WILL-PLAY AWARD for sharing her musical talents when Joan Harris and Bud Farrar were both away; Amos Ticehurst received the LONGEST ARM AWARD for years of faithful service as an usher; Alice Wright walked off with the ALICE TENNEY MEMORIAL "JUST DESSERTS" AWARD for serving thousands of desserts at countless church suppers over the years; and Asa Derrick garnered the coveted GOLDEN TRASHBAG AWARD for saving the church money by picking up the church and parsonage garbage each week. Between the North Hartland and White River Junction churches, ten volunteer leaders were recognized, appreciated, thanked, and applauded. The cost was about three dollars for certificates and about half an hour to type out the certificates.

Volunteers thrive on appreciation—especially genuine appreciation that grows out of relationship. But there is something

else revealed in the award ceremonies that is very important
in leading the small church. Very few of the people who
were recognized would normally be thought of as *leaders*. Yet
they are! Sad to say, *we have accepted a picture of management as a
substitute for leadership*. We look at Asa Derrick with his
GOLDEN TRASHBAG AWARD in his hand, and we wonder what leadership there is in picking up a few bags or
barrels of rubbish. We ask how Jessie Peoples with her
PAUL'S EPISTLE AWARD is a leader. We wonder how
people can be called leaders when they have not even one
person *under them* to manage and order around. *And that is
exactly where the difficulty lies!* We have come to believe that
leadership, like management, means *over and under*—when in
the relationally based church, leadership means *beside*. Remember the Newton-Lewis clan's reunion (Chapter 3)?
Leadership can be long-term or short-term, traditional or
trainee, official or unofficial (as in the extended family).
*Leadership involves filling roles on behalf of the relational community one
is a part of.* As I mentioned in Chapter 3 (Pastoral Leadership),
*a leader senses the needs of his or her community and helps the community
mobilize to satisfy those needs.* Thus eighty-year-old Jessie Peoples assumes a leadership role and becomes a committee of
one to help the women's group satisfy its need for a consola-
tion-and-congratulations outreach. Asa Derrick sensed the
financial pressures the congregation was feeling, and he
mobilized himself and a friend to meet the need by carting
away the trash (rather than having the church pay to have
it done). Edith Jacobs, who received the GOLDEN HAND-
SHAKE AWARD, is confined to her home as the primary
caregiver for her ninety-two-year-old husband, yet she lines
up greeters and coffee hour hosts by telephone each week.
"One does what one can," someone once told me. That
seems to be the motto for many of these leaders who are not
often thought of as leaders.

Douglas W. Johnson, in his excellent book, *The Care and
Feeding of Volunteers*, writes that " . . . volunteers want to do
something worthwhile for and through the church."[1] John-

son is quite right. But in the small church the volunteer leaders want to do something significant *for that particular church that they are in relationship to.* Though some people wish to make a contribution to the "larger church" (or the church universal), most people simply "want to do a significant and meaningful thing" (as a young Sunday church school superintendent told me). Especially in small churches it seems volunteers' leadership is most often directed toward satisfying the needs of their relational group (small church or extended family).

Since one "does what one can" in an effort to "do a significant and meaningful thing," we need to find ways to *acknowledge* what is significant and meaningful. After all, isn't Asa Derrick's effort to save the church money by collecting the trash "a significant and meaningful thing"? And how about Jessie Peoples in her lonely letter-writing ministry? These people have done a significant and meaningful thing. Their efforts and leadership have made a difference—not only for their church, but in people's lives. If one of the basic longings of human beings is to be significant, to make a difference in the scheme of things, one of the most important tasks of the church is to acknowledge and applaud those people when they succeed at being significant.

Johnson has suggested that the acknowledgment of volunteers involves three components: thanking, recognizing, and respecting (as opposed to taking for granted).[2] All the awards mentioned earlier were handed out with a handshake or a hug and a verbal thank-you. Volunteers were assured that their efforts were not only appreciated, but that they were not taken for granted. (Too many churches and pastors seem to think "one does what one can" means "one does what one ought to.") A Vermont bumper sticker reads: KIDS LOVE PRAISE—EVERY DAY. Volunteers love praise regularly, too. Rather than complain about the lack of volunteer leaders, we need to spend more time acknowledging and appreciating them for the significant and meaningful things they do. Once we do that, a flood of creative energy

is released that spurs people on to risk trying another significant and meaningful thing. If each layperson feels he or she
is significant and appreciated in relation to his or her small
church, the church will have no shortage of leadership. Its
laity will be both tuned-in and turned-on.

I once served as an interim pastor in a small church in the
western mountains of Maine. One Sunday I preached about
the need for an access ramp for the church. I mentioned the
names of two persons (with prior permission) who could not
get into the church without assistance. The sermon did not
use guilt as a motivator. It simply spelled out the need and
voiced the feelings of those who felt excluded by the
church's architecture. I also voiced the frustration of the
board of trustees who were faced with budget constraints.
(The church was trying to raise the money to go from a
half-time minister back to a full-time minister.)

After the service, as I shook hands with people on their
way out, a lady handed me a check for one hundred dollars
to get the ball rolling. Several others said they would contribute. But the best part came when a man walked up to me
with his fifteen-year-old son. He said, "We'd like to build
that ramp. My son needs a community service project so he
can get an Eagle Scout badge, and so do several of his
friends. My family has been here a good many years, and
we'd like to do something meaningful for our church. We'll
cut up the lumber right on our land; we'll mill it down the
road; and the Eagle Scouts will build the ramp."

The board of trustees worked jointly with the excited
builders, and the best spot for the ramp was selected. I kept
in close contact with the man and his son, made sure to
include ramp updates in the weekly bulletin and newsletter,
and enlisted people to organize a ramp dedication ceremony.
One of our members, because of disintegrating bone in his
knees, began using a wheelchair while the ramp was under
construction. He agreed to cut the ribbon and ride his wheelchair down the ramp, crashing through a wall of cardboard
bricks to symbolize our church breaking down the barriers

of inaccessibility. Handshakes and certificates went to the designers and builders (in their Eagle Scout uniforms). Pictures were taken. The women's group held a tea party afterwards. But perhaps the best part was that a man who had not been very active of late internalized the needs of his four primary relationship groups—extended family, church, the Eagle Scout troop he led, and community—and he assumed a leader's role in helping to satisfy their needs. He and his group did a meaningful and significant thing. In return, the church and I acknowledged his efforts by recognizing him, thanking him, and by not taking him for granted. Less than a month later he and the Eagle Scouts built a lovely new closet for the choir's robes. One does what one can.

In the late seventies a popular televangelist sent out lapel pins as part of a promotion. The heart-shaped pins proclaimed YOU ARE LOVED. I disliked the passive use of the verb because there was no subject doing the loving. Was the implication "*God* loves you"? Or was it "*Jesus* loves you"? Maybe "*I* love you"? It's important to state *who* loves you.

When my daughter comes to me feeling shaky or insecure, I never say, "You are loved." She needs to hear that *I* love her, and she needs to know that my love is *present* and *active.* "You are loved" is filled with doubt, because it turns the statement into a question: "*Who* loves?" It does nothing to calm our insecurity.

Small churches often feel insecure. Like teenagers, they may be involved in an identity search much of the time. Bigger kids (larger churches or denominations) threaten them and add to their feelings of insecurity. They are sometimes told it isn't right to be who they are, that they must change to be acceptable. "Aw, grow up!" (How many churches feel they've got to measure up on the large church scale?) They are often apologetic about who they are or what they do. Perhaps the most desperate need of small churches today is to be told by their pastors, "I LOVE YOU." They have too often been jilted by pastors who have used them as stepping-stones. They have had their self-esteem damaged by unfair comparisons to their bigger sistren and brethren churches (who also woo their pastors away). They have been made to feel inadequate with regard to mission giving and stewardship of money. They often feel like beggars at the feet of their denominations, picking over what's left or waiting for hand-me-downs to fill pastoral vacancies. Small churches don't feel first-class in many ways. But when it comes to relational strength they can compete with any-one—especially if they can love a pastor who loves them.

Abraham Maslow suggests that motivation is based on a hierarchy of needs, each of which must be met as it comes up in the sequence. The order: (1) physiological needs (such as food, warmth, sex, and elimination); (2) safety needs (security and freedom from fear); (3) social needs (belonging); (4) self-esteem needs; (5)self-realization needs (fulfill-ment).[3] With the increased cost of just surviving as a small church (the number of pledging units necessary to support a church with a full-time minister is much higher than it was in the 1950s), many formerly secure and active small churches have had to shift their focus back to meeting the first need—survival. But more money spent on survival means less money spent on satisfying the second need—security. That's where it is crucial for pastors to transmit a clear message that says "I love you." Once the basic survival needs have been met or will be met (Maslow's first), and the congregation feels secure in its relationship with the pastor (Maslow's second), the social needs (Maslow's third) start getting met. It's then that the small church really gels and leadership emerges. A sense of *who* and a sense of *worth* (Maslow's fourth: self-esteem) become clearer. Out of that identity—with loving, believing pastoral and lay leadership that is sensitive to the body's needs and that works to find ways to satisfy those needs—a sense of purpose becomes more visible. It is then that the small church finds itself involved in self-actualization (though few get there).

One of my field education students at Andover Newton Theological School asked me, "Is it really *that* important to tell them you love them?" Absolutely. As Joel C. Hunter so aptly put it in a recent article for *Leadership* magazine: "Pastoring a church is not so much operating a machine as courting a sweetheart."[4]

Another student asked me, "How often should you tell them?" I answered that I don't just say "I love you" to my wife on Valentine's Day, our anniversary, her birthday, and Mother's Day. I tell her and show her often. Special days are good reminders, but the message needs to be broadcast in many ways on many days. Small churches never tire of hearing that their pastor loves them.

There are a number of ways to communicate this message and, in turn, to promote feelings of security. Written and oral communications are the most obvious, but touching and body language are also important. All of these need to be permeated by a sense of genuineness. Small churches can spot hypocrisy a hundred miles off.

Written

The wife of a pastor friend of mine in Texas recently gave birth to a baby boy. A week after the birth, she and her husband received a bankbook in the mail along with a congratulations card from a local bank. The postscript noted that the bank had donated ten dollars to start a savings account for the birthday boy. Needless to say, that bank communicated clearly that it was interested in the couple and their family.

One pastor in upstate New York told me he wished he owned stock in note card companies. Whenever he sees a news item about a parishioner or a parishioner's relative, he dashes off a short note and drops it in the mail. "I saw in the news that Rick placed third in the YMCA diving meet. You must be proud. Tell Rick I said hello and congratulations."*

---

*I also send out cards, but not as frequently as the pastor from upstate New York. I recently sent one that simply said: "Was driving past your place the other day and saw the new rail fence around the front yard. It really looks great!" A week later I drove past again and noticed that the fence was around the front yard *of the house next door.* My parishioner and I laugh about my mistake every time we see each other.

I discovered the impact of a pastor's written words when I was serving a small church as a student pastor. An eight-year-old girl had sung her first solo before the congregation, so I sent her a thank-you note. Two weeks later, when I went to visit the family, she was playing in the front yard and ran to my car to greet me. When I asked if she had gotten my note, she pulled the well-creased card and envelope out of her back pocket. She'd been carrying it with her all week! Until then I hadn't really understood what an important figure a pastor is in a community or the impact of the pastor's words on a little girl's life.

It's also possible to write an "I love you" pastoral letter that can be mailed *en masse* to the entire congregation. Here is a letter that generated tremendous positive response (financial and verbal) from my parish. It was typed and reproduced on nice Thanksgiving stationery with a Thanksgiving offering envelope enclosed. We bulk mailed it in a business-sized envelope with a Thanksgiving design to match the letterhead.

November 7, 1984

Beloved,
Another Thanksgiving is upon us! But it isn't the roast turkey and dressing and fixings I'm thankful for—it's you! Elizabeth Barrett Browning once wrote, "How do I love thee? Let me count the ways." Well, how do I thank thee all? Let me list a couple of things:
Thanks for attending meetings,
for being patient with my worship leadership,
for your support when my Mom died,
for mothering me at times,
for fathering me at times,
for paying me regularly,
for putting so much money into the church this
year,
for putting so much money outside it this year,

for reaching outward in ministry instead of inward,
for laughing at my jokes,
for welcoming my family and friends who visited,
for taking the pressure off when I was overloaded,
for the rug, the recliner, the afghan, the food,
for calling me your pastor,
for sharing intimately with me,
for sharing your lives and deaths with me,
for patting me on the back often,
for sharing your precious time,
for revealing God to me without realizing it,
for coming to Sunday worship when you can.
Bob Hope's theme song has always been: "Thanks for
the Memories," but I think I'd sing it more like,
"Thanks for the Ministries." This Thanksgiving I'm especially thankful for each of you.

Faithfully,
Steve Burt

P.S. One-half of the money received in the Thanksgiving offering envelopes will go to OxFam (Ethiopian
Famine Relief) and one-half to White River Community Suppers program.

Oral

About every six weeks I preach a sermon that allows me
to tell the congregation how wonderful and worthwhile
they are. I praise their efforts and I may even tell them flat
out that I love them. Too few congregations hear this from
their pastors, and too many hear cold-tongue-and-grumble
soup instead. Here is a Thanksgiving sermon that falls into
the upbuilding category. It is reprinted from *Pulpit Digest.*

"Let's Thank God . . . For the Turkeys
We've Been Given"[5]

Judging from the sermon title, you'd expect I might
talk about our turkey suppers during the foliage season

in Vermont, and their success at fund-raising. Or you might expect I'd say a word of thanks for the turkeys that were donated by people for those suppers. Well, I'm thankful for all that and more, but today I'm referring to different kinds of turkeys. I'm talking about *people*. People turkeys.

Turkeys is a word we hear a lot nowadays—on TV shows, in the slang jive talk of our kids, in everyday speech at work. Somebody will say, "Oh, man, that guy's a real turkey." Or the kids will say it about a school teacher they think is "square" (to use another older slang word): "Oh, Jeez, I got Mr. Kilroy for a homeroom teacher this year; he's a real turkey." Or in hiring someone for a job, we might look at a totally unqualified applicant, someone who doesn't even approach the list of qualifications, and we'll say, "My gosh, what a turkey!"

There's no definition in Webster's dictionary yet, but I'd submit that we look at a turkey like this: as someone who does not remotely fill the bill, as a person who looks like a square peg in a round hole. Got the picture?

In today's Gospel reading from John 17, Jesus is praying for his disciples. He knows he is headed for disaster in Jerusalem because he's been stepping on too many toes, upsetting the *status quo*. He's a threat.

But he has grown to love this band of men. They've shared a lot of meals and a lot of ministry together, as we have here in our church. He has learned to care very deeply for each of them. He is worried about what will happen to them. In Jesus' prayer, one of the most touching in the Bible, he asks God for their safekeeping—but he also *commends* their actions and their spirit.

In effect, he gives thanks to God for them. But let's look at who he is giving thanks for.

Peter, the big impetuous fellow who acted on emotion, put his mouth, fists, and sword into action before engaging his brain. He will cut off a guard's ear at the Garden of Gethsemane, so Jesus will have to reattach it and say, "Peter, let's be cool." Peter is the one who blurts out, "You are the Christ" about Jesus, only to deny him three times later. What a turkey this fellow is!

How about James and John, the sons of Zebedee? In the first chapter of Mark we read: "When Jesus had gone a little farther, he saw James and John, the sons of Zebedee, in a boat, preparing their nets. Without delay he called them, *and they left their father Zebedee in the boat* with the hired servants and followed him." These two young men deserted their Dad to join a traveling evangelist named Jesus! They left Dad right in the middle of work! Can you believe that? What a couple of irresponsible. . . .

And in Mark 10:37 these two, James and John, ask who will be granted the position at Jesus' left hand and who at his right hand in his glory! And at other times they argue among themselves who among them is the greatest! What turkeys!

There is Judas, who sells out for a handful of silver. He was a turkey if ever there was one.

And consider them as a group of disciples. When Jesus says, "Feed the 5,000," how do they respond? They say, "Lord, it's suppertime, and we've only got a couple of bucks for hamburgers. How about if you stand up and command the crowds to go to town and hit the Seven-Elevens and deli counters? We've barely got enough food for ourselves."

This group sure has human failings and imperfections, don't they? This group, with no Dale Carnegie courses or public speaking experience, is expected to preach to the multitudes. This group, with no formal training or schooling, with no seminary experience, is expected to teach people about God. But we can easily see they're only a group of fishermen, tax collectors, and carpenters—no college grads among them. If "turkeys" are defined as people who don't remotely fill the bill, as square pegs in round holes—then Jesus certainly got a bunch of turkeys for disciples, didn't he?

But despite all their boo-boos, despite all their rashness and brashness, despite all their impetuousness, selfishness, and lack of faith, despite their blindness—*despite the fact that they were turkeys when it came to being disciples*—JESUS LOVED THEM. Jesus loved them very deeply.

Listen again to Jesus' prayer for them. I've translated it very loosely from the Greek. "Father, I pray to you for these people, these disciples whom I love; I am not now praying for the saving of the whole world, but specifically for the safety of this group which you have given me out of the world, for they are *yours,* and they have served me honorably, and with faith. Now I am no longer to be a part of the world physically, but they have to stay in this world while I return to you. Holy Father, bless and keep them, this band of disciples you gave me, and by your power help them to remain as one, just as you and I are one."

Jesus uttered a beautiful and genuine prayer *for a bunch of turkeys!* Jesus didn't pray for better-equipped disciples or for replacements! Jesus gave thanks to God for the people God had given him. And he loved them. Sure, sometimes it was one step ahead and two back. But mostly it was two ahead and one back. And they got the job done.

One of the most frequently heard comments pastors hear is this: "We've got to attract some new blood to this church." It is a statement built on the misconception that there is someone else who can do it better than I can, or better than we can. That is partly a self-image problem.

It can be heard in subtle variations, too: "Maybe we can get that new couple in town to come to church. They're young. And after they're in, maybe they'll agree to teach Sunday school." Or: "Maybe we can get

Jane Jones to teach church school. After all, she's a *professional* teacher." Can you hear it in there? "Someone else can do it better than us."

If it were put in the form of a prayer, it might sound like this: "O Lord, give us newer, better, fresher people."

In many crumbling churches it is carried to its extreme, and it comes out like this: "O Lord, we've only got a bunch of turkeys left here, square pegs for round holes. How do you expect us to get the job done?"

Lest pastors be forgotten, there is a special version which they utter, but it boils down to the same thing: "If we only had more dedicated Christians like John and Mary Smith, maybe this church wouldn't be in so much trouble."

And the stewardship chairperson says it like this: "If we only had more ten-percent tithers and fewer one dollar tippers, we wouldn't have to sweat the budget each year."

The choir director: "If we only had more trained voices in the choir, we could sing louder, better, and with more inspiration."

The women's group says: "If only we had more younger women, we could support more bazaars, have more suppers, put on more rummage sales."

Folks, Jesus Christ didn't look for replacements. And Jesus Christ didn't send people back to God for an exchange. Jesus Christ gave humble and heartfelt thanks for the turkeys God had given him out of the world— for the ill-fitting square pegs who had to do round-hole jobs. Today is a good time to give thanks, and I am thankful for all of you turkeys who are here today, and for those turkeys who couldn't be with us. We don't have to pray for replacements. We've got you, and I'm thankful. Our Sunday schools have outstanding turkeys teaching them. They aren't professional teachers, so I suppose that makes them square pegs in round holes, but they all *care* and they *dare* to express their faith with the kids.

And maybe everyone isn't as dedicated as John and Mary Smith, the ideal Christian couple, but dedication tends to come and go at different times in life, influenced by many factors. It can diminish or grow for any of us over the years. And not everyone *should* be like John and Mary. It would be boring.

We also don't need a bunch of new people to fill the pews, or to get use from the building, or to float the budget, or to feel we're doing a good job as a church. We turkeys are the ones who are *right here, right now.* And if you check, you'll see the budget *is* making it, and the church *is* alive—not because of an influx of newcomers, but because of the work, and money, and dedication of the turkeys, the square pegs—the cooks, waiters, and waitresses who aren't *really* cooks, waiters, and waitresses, but who do those jobs here anyway; the teachers and singers who aren't professional teachers and singers; the host of others who do the job anyway.

Our choir doesn't have professional voices, or opera singers, or a professional director—but our choir sings, and inspires, and has great fellowship.

Our women's group, without a whole bunch of replacements for their older women, still puts on bazaars, is having lunches, meetings, and rummage sales, and provides the fellowship that is so vital to so many women. It's not necessary to have *more* bazaars, *more* suppers, *more* sales.

Our budget is afloat and working, not because of new donors, but because of all of us turkeys who believe in the work and mission of Jesus Christ.

If turkeys are square pegs in round holes, if turkeys are people who don't remotely fill the bill, if turkeys are the least likely disciples—then I guess you and I are turkeys, so we may as well own up to it. The last thing I expected to be in life was a pastor, and here I am. For all you turkeys, let's stop talking about replacing or supplementing with others who can do a better job, with others who are "more qualified." *God has given us whom God has given us.* That's why it's working now— because of turkeys. As Jesus' disciples, let's face it, we're all a bunch of turkeys. And we already have too many pastors whose attitudes toward their people have gone sour. I can appreciate and feel very deeply the prayer Jesus offered, and I am thankful for you people whom God has given me to care about, and to share my ministry with. May God bless and keep you. Amen.

Touching and Body Language

Dr. Walter Cook, retired field education director at Bangor (Maine) Theological Seminary, taught me basic pastoral touching and body language. It was Walter who got me to stop sitting with my arms folded across my chest in church board meetings. It was Walter who taught me the warmth of a two-handed handshake. And it was also Walter who taught me not to grip too firmly because many older parishioners had arthritis in their fingers and preferred pastors with a sensitive grip. But perhaps the most valuable lesson he taught me about touching was based around an immersion baptism I was asked to do for a woman. (It was to have taken place in a fire pond between the church and the firehouse, but the talk of leeches later convinced her to be sprinkled instead.)

Since I had never been faced with an immersion baptism, I went to Walter to learn about the technique. Technique was my main concern. So Walter demonstrated several possible techniques for me in his office. But seeing the confusion on my face, he said, "All this doesn't matter a hang. The only thing she'll remember out of the whole baptism is whether or not your hand is behind the small of her back and she feels secure when you lean her back. And that's the most important thing, isn't it—that she feels she can trust you to let her down into the water and get her back up? It's the feeling of trust she'll recall, not the technique." Walter Cook was right. Our body language and our touch speak our message as loudly and clearly as our mouths, and maybe more so.

All this talk of hoopla, appreciation, recognition, respect, affirmation, security, and unabashed affection may seem simplistic in the face of the flyers promising guaranteed-to-work church growth programs (complete with blueprints for recruiting and training volunteers). But it is not simplistic. It is simple. It is simple and basic, and maybe that's why we forget to do it anymore. We think we can forget the basics of developing and cultivating human relationships. But we can't. And if we can get back to the basics of paying attention to people, it is the people who will respond.

6

"What Can Our Small Church Do?"

When folks hear that I'm big on small churches, they corral me to pick my brain about *their* small churches. "What can our small church do?" they often ask. After I've made sure it's not a case of the small church blues ("What can our *small* church do?") nor a rhetorical question ("What can *any* small church do today in the face of . . . ?"), but that it is a genuine search for mission, ministry, and program ideas ("What can *our* church *do?*"), I answer honestly, "I don't know."

I *don't* know. Honestly. Each small church is unique and different. Each has its own needs, resources, history, style, purpose, and context. But while I can't suggest specifics for each church, I can suggest a dozen guidelines to help leaders as they look at their small church's ministry, mission, and programming.

1. *Content must be relative to context.* Programming doesn't happen in a vacuum. It is in relation to a specific place, time, and set of circumstances. What works famously in one church may flop royally in the church just down the road.

For example, the church in White River Junction (Vermont) started The Second Hand Rose Shop, a good quality, low-cost used clothing ministry. The women's group knew that the local community action agency also ran a thrift shop with tons of used clothing people could sort through. But the women also knew that many people who wouldn't go to the Community Action thrift store would come to their Second Hand Rose—if used clothing was of good quality, if it was attractively displayed, and if it was sorted and priced. In polling the congregation and community, they found many people would be willing to donate nearly new clothing that they would hesitate to donate to the Community Action thrift store. The women's group also knew they had plenty of space in the parish hall, because the church school had shrunk with the passing of the baby boom years. They also had a number of retired women who said they would like to work in pairs on Wednesday and Saturday afternoons. The program has been wonderfully successful in many ways—financially for the church, in offering low-cost quality clothing to the community, and in providing a creative outlet for a number of workers who wish to donate their time to the church. (A number of families also have been clothed free due to extreme need.) The Second Hand Rose used clothing ministry is programmatic *content* in relation to *context*.

But to illustrate the importance of reading the context, the same idea was tried in a more rural town only ten miles away—and it failed miserably.

2. *The program or ministry must address real needs.* This is closely related to the context/content question.

Our church answered an ad in the newspaper for a free hospital bed to be given away. We planned to store it for later sale at our annual church auction, but someone suggested we make it available for free loan to anyone who needed it. We advertised it in our church newsletter. Almost immediately it was loaned out to someone with debilitating arthritis. Because of the person's need, the women's group purchased a recliner for loan to the same person. After six months both were returned with thanks, and the recliner went out again after two weeks (to a man recovering from a prostate problem; he needed a comfortable chair). We also bought a wheelchair for fifty dollars through a newspaper ad, and it was on loan within a week. Since then people have donated walkers (each worth about seventy dollars), three-pronged and four-pronged aluminum canes, shower seats, a special toilet seat that is high and has side grips, two more hospital beds, another wheelchair, and a variety of canes and crutches. We have found the hospital equipment loan program meets so many needs that we now keep a log book for checking things in and out.[1]

3. *Seek input from a wide cross section of the church and community.* The leaders need not be the only ones to identify needs or to suggest possible programs and ministries. By soliciting (and taking seriously) the suggestions of the whole body, a broader spectrum of needs becomes evident, and access to more ideas and suggestions for meeting those needs becomes available.

One church printed visitor cards to place in their pews, and on the last line asked: "What can we do to help you feel more comfortable with us?" Someone wrote: "First, give me a pencil to write this answer with; second, give directions to the bathroom; third, tell me where to find the collection song."

The church had seriously asked for input, and they got it. A task force began identifying barriers to newcomers, and came up with an extensive list.

a. Shop talk. Too much in-house language like PPRC (Pastor-Parish Relations Committee) that tended to exclude outsiders.

b. A worship bulletin designed for insiders. There was always an asterisk next to certain words (*Hymn or *Gloria Patri), but no explanation of what the asterisk indicated (* means congregation please stand). There was no hint of where to find words for the Doxology, the Gloria Patri, the Lord's Prayer, or the Response to the Benediction.

c. Inaccessibility for the physically disabled. There was no ramp or elevator. Only a willingness to help carry a wheelchair-bound person up the steps, which a wheelchair-bound person told the task force was unacceptable.

d. Inaccessibility to the sermon for hearing-impaired worshipers.

e. Lack of large-print or Braille Bibles, hymnals, and worship bulletins for the sight-impaired and blind.

f. Lack of visitor and handicapped parking spaces/signs.

g. No clear times, addresses, or phone numbers for church school, morning worship, adult classes, personnel, and so forth.

h. No signs or directions to indicate the location of offices and rest rooms.

i. Poor condition of welcome/directional signs to the church from town borders.

j. No pencils in pews.

A number of other issues were identified later, but the initial ten gave the church something to work on. An elevator was installed; large-print Bibles were purchased; a special system for the hearing-impaired was looked into; new signs (directional, handicapped, and visitor) were purchased; the bulletin was completely reworked for clarity for newcomers; rest room and office signs were added; the church's front sign (and the heading of the morning bulletin) was sharpened to provide helpful information such as times and phone numbers; sharp pencils and plenty of visitor cards graced the pews each week. In addition, the church members began to wear name tags at Sunday morning worship to make newcomers more comfortable. All because the church solicited input beyond its own leadership team.

4. *Use people's talents and gifts.* People are the greatest resource the small church has. A church on eastern Long Island (N.Y.) found that two of its parishioners were registered nurses who were concerned about people's blood pressure. The two nurses brought in blood pressure cuffs three or four times a year so they could check and record blood pressures. Their ministry provided a helpful service (especially for the elderly) and made good use of available talents.

5. *Be on the lookout for ideas easily translated or adapted from one small church context to another.* There are many church-related magazines that contain sections for exchanging ideas or "it-worked-for-us" information. Some churches exchange newsletters in order to share ideas. Although The Second Hand Rose used clothing ministry wasn't easily translatable from White River Junction church to the church down the road, the blood pressure clinic would be fairly easy to do in almost any church. (Someone other than a registered nurse could be taught to do it.) Many of the best ministry and program ideas are borrowed.

6. *Be realistic.* This especially applies to financial and human resources. Being realistic (for example, trying to keep up with Old First Church downtown) can lead to frustration and burnout. With esteem such a problem nowadays, small church folks need to experience more successes.

Over the 1980 Labor Day weekend, a group of ladies took turns serving free hot coffee and homemade doughnuts at a rest area along the Maine turnpike. They didn't hand out tracts or employ buttonhole evangelism. They just offered cheery conversation and refreshment to weary weekend travelers. The banner flapping in front of their table identified them as the Ladies Aid Society of a local Congregational church, and its bold letters proclaimed WE CARE. But what was amazing was that they represented only an eighty-member church! Who can say how many accidents were avoided or how many lives were saved by their efforts? They were realistic in their roadside ministry. A few cans of coffee, doughnuts solicited throughout their community, and eight cheerful women engaged in small church ministry and witness.

7. *Be creative.* All ministry ideas need not be borrowed or adapted. New program and outreach ideas are constantly being discovered or developed, and they need to be shared.

The women's group in White River Junction served a prewedding feast to five engaged couples, all of whom would be married between March 31 and August 4, 1984.

Only one of the brides and none of the grooms had any previous connection with the church. And even though several of the couples had lived together, the women's group said their message was, "We heartily affirm you in your decisions to wed. We're not here to judge you, but to affirm you (and feed you)."

The five couples who formed the group had not known one another before, but they had found something in common: wedding plans and nervousness. Some of them (it was found out later) prayed for the success of one another's wedding days. The church has had a difficult time attracting young adults in recent years. They would come to morning worship, look around, see they were in the minority, and leave. The prewedding feast helped form a common bond among the couples, encouraging them to enter the membership *en masse.* [2] In the year that followed, two couples did in fact become involved in the church—one of the brides converting from Judaism a year after her wedding day. She received adult baptism one week, and her newborn son received infant baptism the next week. The women's group is planning another meal, this one to involve couples who were married at the church in the past three years. They can eat, share slides, and swap stories. Be creative in programming!

8. *Balance output with intake.* Doctors are forever reminding us that we need both exercise *and* diet. If we only take in—but fail to exercise—we get fat. Then we are likely to develop hardening of the arteries. In churches that translates to hardness of heart. On the other hand, if we only exercise without eating, we get thin and nervous. Churches experience this as exhaustion and volunteer burnout. Too much emphasis on one or the other can lead to spiritual death.

Some programs are heavy on the feeding or ingestion aspect, as with study and discussion groups. Other programs require mostly output, as with operating a secondhand clothing ministry or a soup kitchen. The church school teacher who never gets to attend worship may need an opportunity for nourishment in the face of so much demand for output. That may mean providing a substitute once a month or having teachers only serve three-month terms. Or it more likely reveals the need to offer an adult study class at a time the teacher can participate for spiritual intake. As in the needs of the individual teacher, the entire church needs to have access to a balanced program of output and intake.

9. *Ministry and programs need to be in line with the church's purpose and goals.* While the church's overall purpose may be as simple a statement as "to meet needs and to make the good news of Jesus Christ accessible to all," the goal might be broken into smaller, more concrete, more measurable goals. For example, one church listed as part of its goal "to be as receptive as possible to newcomers by working hard to be seen by them as the friendliest and most approachable church in town." They began to wear name tags at morning worship and placed the following announcement in the morning bulletin (as a message to visitors, but also to keep the purpose and goals in front of current members): "We members and friends of the Church of the Open Arms wear name tags in an effort to go beyond a handshake to visitors and new attenders. We hope our efforts make getting acquainted easier for everyone."

10. *Prioritize programs and resources.* No church can expect to meet all the needs around it. Decisions need to be made by the church (not just by the pastor or by the treasurer) about which needs can and will be addressed when, in what order, how, by whom, and with what resources.

"Can we afford the extra heating and lighting costs if we set up a soup kitchen in our church?"

"How will a small church like ours staff a soup kitchen? Can we get other churches to help us?"

"How often will we feed? One meal a week? two? five?"

"Where will we get the food? From the government? private donations? fresh produce in season? local restaurants?"

"What will be the wear and tear on our facility? on the new rug the women's group had installed? on our dishes and pots and pans? Maybe there's a better place in town to hold a soup kitchen."

"Are there really hungry people in our area?"

"Would we be better off donating to a nearby soup kitchen and putting our energy into the shelter for the homeless that the Catholic and Episcopal churches are trying to get going?"

All these questions are part of a church's process of prioritizing—making tough decisions as to how we can best be responsible stewards while doing our best to meet the needs around us.

11. *Build in recognition, acknowledgment, and appreciation.* Schedule times along the way for celebrations, time-outs, hoopla, and promotions. One pastor and her church school teachers go out for lunch (on the church) at the end of the first two church school quarters. They relax, swap stories, and wind down as they prepare to get wound up again. And they know the church appreciates them enough to buy lunch. (In another small church in New York State, a church member takes the entire choir out to dinner at a steak house every year to show his appreciation of their efforts.)

In the town of Hartford (Vermont), the soup kitchen is staffed by ten feeding teams of three to six people per team. Every four months everyone gets together for a pot luck supper and an awards ceremony. Some of the handmade awards (construction paper) are humorous and some are serious, but they all are given out of deep appreciation for service and sacrifice. There is much applause. Participation and the chances of a program's success are increased by planning that builds in recognition, acknowledgment, and appreciation from the very start.

12. *Plan to evaluate and review.* Build checkpoints into the program with opportunities for midcourse corrections. This means planning beforehand how reliable feedback and relevant data will be gathered. Statistics at certain points on a time continuum might include money received, people fed, meals prepared, visits made, lessons taught, and so forth.

Data is important in evaluating and reviewing programs along the way.

Gut feelings are important, too, because *feelings are facts.* Feelings are relevant data, especially in a relational organization like the small church. A church in New Hampshire organized a parent helper program that met in their parish hall. Its purpose was to provide good role models (volunteers from the church and community) who would interact in a preschool setting with young mothers who lacked good parenting skills. When it came to the end of the first six months it was time for program review and evaluation. The data on numbers of volunteers participating, numbers of families served, satisfaction of families served, and most everything else was very promising.

But several people wanted an end to the program. They moaned and groaned about wear and tear on the building, extra heating costs, and the fact that none of the program's recipients of services ever darkened the door of the church. After some skillful diplomacy on the part of the pastor, the real reason for their displeasure came out. One of them had been treated rudely by a young mother who insisted on parking in the parish hall driveway! The young mother had come to the church for free services, never contributed to the church in any way, and dared to offer a member a tongue-lashing! Cancel that program! Off with its head! In checking the feedback during program evaluation, remember—feeling are facts.

Another important point about evaluation and review: don't evaluate the program in a vacuum, and don't evaluate it only for one value. Evaluate in relation to the overall purpose, goals, and programs of the church. Many programs overlap in their values and purposes.

For example, paid public suppers are often evaluated harshly on only one point—money. (This is voiced as "Everyone ought to tithe ten percent in church.") That doesn't take into consideration that church suppers have evolved as a way of meeting *multiple needs* and promoting *multiple values.*

Church suppers encourage fellowship and community building. They provide high visibility for the church in the community. Church suppers foster teamwork and cooperation, and they build self-esteem by enabling the less fortunate to give in food or service. Because of their intergenerational nature, the modeling that occurs at church suppers ("It's good to serve the church") is solid Christian education for the youth. Church suppers promote healing by giving the grieving work to do and relationships to deepen. They provide a low-cost family night out for those who could not otherwise afford it, or for those who could not face another night of cooking and washing dishes. Church suppers encourage inclusion of peripheral members and nonmembers who may become more active later in other areas of church life. If dinners are delivered to shut-ins, the church's visitation ministry is strengthened. And regarding the money question, monies for survival, mission, and ministries are provided (as with the baked bean fund-raising supper for the family burned out in Chapter 1). Hungry famine-stricken Ethiopians don't ask whether their food was paid for with tithed money or church supper proceeds![3] Avoid the temptation to evaluate programs on just a one-point basis. But do seek feedback and evaluate them all along the way.

What can our small church do? I still don't know. Not exactly. But I do know there is plenty that each small church *can* do, given its unique context, needs, people, and resources. May God bless us with wisdom, patience, and discernment as we small churches seek to minister in Christ's name.

Stalking the Small Church Pastor: Before the Hunt Begins

Some anonymous wit has written:

> "The results of a computerized survey indicate that the perfect small church pastor preaches exactly fifteen minutes, condemning sin but never upsetting anyone. He works from 8 A.M. until midnight, makes fifty dollars a week, wears good suits, buys good books, drives a good car, and gives about fifty dollars a week to the poor. The perfect small church pastor is twenty-eight years old and has been preaching for twenty-five years. He has a burning desire to work with teenagers and loves to spend all his time with senior citizens. The perfect small church pastor makes fifteen calls daily on parish families, shut-ins, and the hospitalized. He spends all his time evangelizing the unchurched, and is always available in his office when needed."

We laugh at what seems to be an impossible job description, but the truth is: impossible expectations really are placed on small church pastors, not only during their tenure, *but also long before the search committee even begins to prepare the church's profile or starts sifting through resumes.* Each congregation has a pastoral caricature that is a mishmash of the group's individual and collective expectations (based on wants, needs, experiences, and myths). But seldom do these expectations get put down on paper. More often they are voiced when it is too late—when the pastor's resignation is being demanded.

Just consider the characters who make up the search committee for Ourtown Community Church. Widow Dantley *hopes* for a young pastor who will be successful (where everyone else has failed) in keeping the town's youth off the streets (and inside the church somewhere). Zealous Deacon Burnside *dreams* of doubling the church membership to 500 (even though the town of 450 has been declining in population at 5 percent annually for over a decade). Ben and Serena Lewis *need* a good marriage counselor. Thad and Eleanor Kryloff (known locally as the "Cry-a-lots") *remember* the "baby boom" years and want another Rev. Spurrier who "had this church packed for three services every Sunday" (and whose sermons are still remembered by most people as only fair). As we might guess, most church/pastor mismatches often have little to do with "bad" churches or "incompetent" pastors. Instead, the problem is often that expectations based on hopes, dreams, needs, and memories are not spelled out, and the church does not provide a unified picture of what their pastoral needs are. There are, however, several things that can be done to better the odds of a good church/pastor match. One is to use better interviewing techniques (to be discussed in the next chapter). But several other things need to be done *before* the hunt begins.

A husband and wife sat in their Maine living room. He looked up from his newspaper and said, "Honey, tomorrow I'm going out to shoot me a moose."

"I ain't cooking no moose," she answered sharply. "It's too darned big for my skillet."

The husband scratched his head, thought for a moment, and said, "Then how about a rabbit? A rabbit will match your skillet fine."

"Nope," she said firmly. "Rabbit *fits* okay, but rabbit don't *set right* with me. A fat pheasant would fit the skillet and taste good, too."

Next day the husband went out and shot a pheasant, and he and his wife lived happily ever after.

Small churches too often panic when it's time to fill a pastoral vacancy. The PASTOR WANTED shingle gets hung out, inviting all comers. Such an approach isn't much different from deciding to shoot a moose before sizing up the skillet or before polling others in the household of faith to see what would "set right." A large church pastor in a small church could be a moose in a skillet. But even hiring a small church pastor for a small church won't guarantee that he or she will "set" any better than the rabbit set for the wife. Small churches need to get a clear fix on their current and future needs by asking questions and by listening. They need to first determine what type of small church pastor they are looking for, and then they need to be able to identify one when they spot him or her.

What's needed is to get from moose to pheasant (as the hunter did), and there are several ways.

First (and most overlooked) is *church and community assessment.* All *goal-setting* begins with "where we are." This means *description* and *analysis.* From there the small church can look at the *direction* it wants to go in relation to its *purpose.* Large churches aren't the only churches that need their direction and purpose updated and clarified from time to time.

One old-timer, when approached with the idea of a church and community assessment, remarked, "That's for them big city churches. They've got a bigger spread to ride herd over."

While his statement about size may be true, small churches still need a sense of direction and purpose, both of which have to be reflected on regularly. If a church knows *who* it is, *what* it is like, *where* it is going, and *why* it needs to get there, it will have a much better idea of its progress at any given time *(when)*.

To illustrate the value of "taking stock," I submit the following article. The names and towns have been changed, but it is based on an article that appeared on the front page of a New England daily newspaper.

CHURCHES IN BLOOMBERG AND ROCKMINSTER MAY CLOSE, MERGE, BUILD NEW ONE[1]

ROCKMINSTER—A proposal to close a 124-year-old church and merge it with a Bloomberg church is being debated in Rockminster.

Members of the United Christian Church in Rockminster attended a public meeting yesterday to discuss the possible merger of their church with the Christian Church in Bloomberg. Under this proposal the two existing buildings would be sold and a new church built in West Rockminster.

The meeting was held during a regular church service and was led by Lois Mills, Colleen Jessup, and Philip Singer, active church members.

It was widely agreed that a lack of membership and support has created the present situation. Mills said, "If all Sunday services were this well-attended we may not have had this problem."

Financial support from members had decreased considerably from last year. "In Easter 1984, $224 was received in pledges as compared to $96 in Easter 1985," said Singer. "Last year we received 22 pledges (of financial support) out of 122 members; this is only 18 percent of our members. Finances are an important part of our church."

Rockminster United Christian Church has ninety-three members. "Only a few do all the work," said Jessup. Jessup said the church should become more active in attracting young people, the future supporters of the church.

One church member, Bloomberg resident Mary

Hutchings, said, "It's a serious reflection on the present leadership of the church to retain its members. If sermons were more inspiring the average United Christian would support the church." In response Singer said, "Jesus Christ could be up here preaching and someone wouldn't like it."

Josh Wright, a church member, said, "There is a lack of church leadership. Ministers go off on tangents and get involved in other things." Wright also suggested the church should consider hiring a professional fundraiser to increase financial support.

"The congregation will work to avoid the merger, but it may have to be," said another church member, Albert Leonard.

"The worst thing that could happen is that the congregation will vote down the merger and then do nothing," said Singer.

Some members expressed concern about the historical value of the church, which was built in 1861. Others found it difficult to justify the cost of building a new church when the present one has no mortgage.

"Will it (the merger) solve our problems? Will we be spending more money to save money?" church organist Barbara Herndon asked rhetorically.

The decision to sell the United Christian Church in Rockminster and merge with the Bloomberg Church will be voted upon at a church conference on May 8. All church members may participate.

The article reveals a major need for assessment and planning. There is clearly a lack of awareness of *who we are* in 1985. (We aren't the same churches we were in 1955.) And it is also clear that the failure to recognize social change (which has led to poor clarity of self-image) is affecting the parish's perceptions of their leaders (primarily the co-pastors). A good church assessment can reveal many things about a church and its community. It might have helped in Rockminster and Bloomberg. Just a few items that can be seen in the one news article:

1. While it was "widely agreed that a lack of membership and support has created the present situation," these are *not* *the cause.* They are *symptoms.* The statement as it stands now puts the blame on *people* for their failure to be numerically and financially supportive. It also blames the *leaders* (both pastoral and lay) for their lack of *commitment* and for their inability to inspire ("If sermons were more inspiring . . . "). The co-pastors are being blamed for what may be unclearly spelled-out priorities of pastors' energies (if ministers didn't "go off on tangents and get involved in other things"). It may be that the ministers were told at their hiring interviews that the church wanted to strengthen its ties to the community, and the pastors are trying to do that.

2. A quick check of an old atlas shows the 1960 Bloomberg population was 1,121 within village limits, but that the township (which the church could draw from) totaled 1,867. A 1985 road map no longer listed Bloomberg.

Rockminster's 1960 census listed 450 in the village and 1,507 for the entire township (which the church could draw from). But the 1985 road map tallied only 780 for the township—half of what it had been!

The closing of the mines and the decline of the local mills (due to foreign competition) had taken its toll—but the changes went unnoticed by the churches! A check of the kindergarten and grade school enrollments might have provided some eye-opening data for a comparison of present numbers of young people to the figures in postwar baby boom years. "Attracting young people, the future supporters of the church," is not primarily a *leadership* problem. It is often a problem of numbers, logistics, and need. When the larger number of community activities for young people is added to the larger number of school sports and events nowadays, the church needs to ask the pertinent question: Is there a need for a youth group (or other program)? At any rate, there is no need for mudslinging and insulting the leadership. Nor is there any reason for congregations to carry loads of guilt for situations caused by social change. (Where they need to be called accountable is in their ignoring of it.) Small churches do need to put things in perspective and go from there.

3. Misunderstood social change has placed extra pressure on pastors and lay leaders ("It's a serious reflection on the present leadership of the church . . . If sermons were more inspiring the average United Christian would support the church.")[2] I suspect the average United Christians *are* supporting these churches, and I believe the sermons are no better or worse than any of the past twenty-five pastors' sermons. For decades the Gallup Poll has found that great preaching is not the prime mover of those who attend worship. In fact, only ten to twenty percent come because of the minister (not even necessarily for his or her preaching). The Gallup Report on Religion in America 1984 showed that a full sixty to ninety percent attended church because their friends or relatives invited them.[3] Another four to ten percent came because of the activities.[4] Taking into consideration the population decline in Rockminster and Bloomberg, the social changes affecting adults and youth (competing activities and less youth available to draw from), and the Gallup data reporting that sermons are not the drawing card we preachers imagine they are—with all these taken into consideration—why blame the leadership?

4. Inflation has hit the church just as it has hit the average family, but the real destructive power of inflation is experienced when we blame the church's financial woes on the commitment (expressed as "lack of") of members or the inability of leaders to lead, and when we are too quickly and so "widely agreed that a lack of membership and support has created the present situation." Hogwash! Clergy salaries have had to go up to keep pace with inflation, and the "cost of doing business" as a church has risen dramatically over the past three decades. Heating the building is no easy mat-

ter, with the cost of petroleum products having quadrupled since 1970. The cost of power has jumped considerably. Pulp product prices (which affect the prices of published church school and worship materials as well as books and toilet paper) have skyrocketed. Insurance costs have risen sharply, both for fire coverage and liability. Once the pastor's salary was the bulk of the annual budget, but current operating expenses may now amount to two or three times the pastor's salary. Most church budgets have more than quadrupled since 1955.

The Rockminster/Bloomberg article contained an often misinterpreted item: the percentage of pledging members. The figure isn't compared to anything (other churches of comparable size, socioeconomic base, past figures). It is simply flung before us. And the statistics can be misleading. In a church of 122 members, perhaps many are families of three or four—so a *family's* pledge may include three or four church members. (*Several* members show up as *one pledging unit.*) If the figures in the article are adjusted for such a reality (if it *is* a reality, then the percentage of faithful pledging members may be over fifty percent! How many members give regularly without wanting to submit a pledge card? Why imply that the church's membership is guilty of a lack of commitment or lack of support? ("This is only eighteen percent of our members.")

By simply taking seriously the impact of inflation, we can relieve some of the members' guilt feelings. Maybe fifteen to twenty pledging units (single people, a couple, a family) could support a small church with a full-time pastor in the 1950s, but it now takes over sixty pledging units to do the same thing! So a church that had fifteen to twenty pledging units in the 1950s needs to have *tripled* in numbers to sustain the same level of pastoral support and programming. Such increased strain is incredible, and without an assessment to help see the real roots of the problems, the blame game starts and many good people get hurt. Once our churches get serious about assessment, it will be easier to plan for and to move toward the future. But until we get serious about some regular checkups, we will continue to unwittingly set up people traps and pastor traps.

5. Unclearly spelled-out priorities for the pastor's time often go hand-in-hand with poor articulation of the church's purpose and goals; these can combine to create major tension between pastor and parish. My hunch would be that the co-pastors serving Rockminster and Bloomberg (there is also a third church at Bloomberg Corners) received signals at their interviews telling them that the churches (wanting to solve the problems created by "lack of membership and support") were interested (1) in reaching beyond their own walls; and (2) in strengthening their ties with the community. But the church's *motive* is often *institutional survival* (more attenders and pledging units to support the budget) while the *co-pastors probably interpreted it to mean increased outreach ministry, or meeting the needs of those beyond the membership!* Crossed signals! Missed communications! All of this is bound to raise Cain with pastoral priorities—especially if one pastor engages in alcohol crisis work and the other in family violence crisis work ("off on tangents and get involved in other things"), neither of which bring much new blood into the church. As a consequence the co-pastors (in a small church where evangelism often necessarily means "signing up" new members for survival's sake), while doing what they *believed* the membership had set as a high priority (community outreach), wind up being condemned by those same members for infidelity (straying too far from the pastor/member relationship). Clear stating of goals, strategies, and priorities can help.

There are several good books available on church assessment, and there are quite a few on church planning and goal setting (assessment needs to come first).[5] But the best route is to employ a reputable church consultant. (Some denominations have a person on staff or available, but an independent consultant does not have the vested interest in a church that a denomination might have.) An outside consultant's job is to discover and point out what the church leadership may be overlooking or misunderstanding—social and demographic change, consistencies/inconsistencies in decision-making, procedure, community view of the church, the church's strong points, and so forth. The object is to get a thorough and honest assessment *from which to plan*. But an assessment is not a plan; it is not answer time, it is checkup time. And it should be done *before* the search committee begins stalking the small church pastor. An assessment is one step that can help get from moose to pheasant.

Churches can also begin the task of assessment themselves, though insiders sometimes can't see the forest for the trees. If the local church is determined to go it themselves, though, the best way to begin is by looking at priorities. This is something that can be started by playing "The Card Game"[6] at the end of the chapter.

"The Card Game" is a tool that can be (1) used to point up the need for assessment and planning; (2) used as a help in goal-setting based on perceived needs that surface, even before a pastoral candidate is sought; (3) included as a part of a structured pastoral interview to help both the pastoral candidate and the parish discover their match/mismatch areas (usually not in the initial interview, but in a later interview); (4) used annually by the pastor and the parish council/board to see and adjust to changing parish needs and priorities. By working out "The Card Game" and listing the results on paper, the impossible caricature of the perfect small church pastor (beginning of chapter) can be eliminated. No pastor could meet all those expectations.

"The Card Game" can help a church *begin* sorting out its hopes, dreams, and needs from its fuzzy memories, competing priorities, and resulting unfair judgments. *For the church* prioritizing means taking itself seriously and taking the pastor seriously. *For the pastor,* prioritizing means taking himself or herself seriously and seeking to be responsive to the church's *self-* identified needs. Not only does this allow pastors to be more human and less caricatured, but many mismatches can be avoided before they occur. (An outreach-to-the-town pastor may decide not to accept a call to a visit-mostly-the-membership church or vice-versa, thereby avoiding a mismatch.) Such responsible action in prioritizing leaves the door open for a more closely matched candidate, a "pheasant" rather than a "rabbit." Though both "fit the skillet," one "sets better."

There is much to be done before the small church hangs out the PASTOR WANTED shingle, just as the husband and wife needed much dialogue to get from moose to pheasant. There needs to be dialogue, question-asking, assessment, planning, goal-setting, and prioritizing. The small church that does at least some of these will be best prepared to invite a qualified and excited candidate into a pastoral interview.

Using the Card Game

It constantly amazes me to hear first-time users of this tool say, "Why Joe, I had no idea *that* was most important for you!" or "I'm surprised to see that less than half of us placed preaching at the top of the list. I had always *assumed*. . . . "

Before using The Card Game, people need to be clear about *how* it will be used and *for what purpose.* It is not a substitute for church planning, but it can be used to expose false assumptions or to point up the need for planning. If planning has already been done (following assessment), the game can be used to help direct a pastor's energies (prioritizing). It can also be used as a means to stimulate discussion of hopes, dreams, and values when the church and candidate meet for an interview. It is often helpful to graph the results so they can be used later on for comparison as needs change.

Instructions

1. First make enough copies so everyone can have a full deck of eleven cards.

The Card Game

COUNSELING—Premarital, marriage, crisis, bereavement, vocational, personal, and spiritual growth. Primarily one-to-one, pastor-to-couple, or pastor-to-family time.	TEACHING—Teaching and supervision of educational ministries. May include teacher training, Christian education meetings, and time spent leading adult classes.
PREACHING AND LEADING WORSHIP—Sermon preparation, worship preparation, administering the sacraments of baptism and the Lord's Supper. Conducting worship.	VISITING—Primarily to visit in the homes of the church and community, especially among the sick, the aged, and others in need. Not visitation of potential members.
EVANGELISM—Calling on potential new members and the unchurched. Includes time spent training laypersons for evangelism.	PERSONAL GROWTH—Time allotted for retreats, reading, seminars for the pastor to develop the spiritual base from which he or she is able to function in other categories. Intake.
MANAGEMENT—Management ministries, meetings, goal-setting, program planning, evaluating. Supervising the church's working program.	LEADERSHIP DEVELOPMENT—Recruiting volunteers and officers, placement, and leadership development.
ADMINISTRATION—Budget, office, church records, property, personal accountability, correspondence, communications. telephone time, mail sorting, ordering books and materials.	ECUMENICAL AND DENOMINATIONAL RESPONSIBILITIES—Local clergy associations in planning and implementing ecumenical events and ministries; serve on denominational committees and attend conferences.
COMMUNITY LEADER—Serving on boards of nonprofit organizations whose goals are in keeping with the purpose of the church. Contributing time to areas where the church can help.	

2. Clarify the question so everyone is responding to the same question. It may be as simple as "What *should* the pastor's priorities be?" or "What *are* they now?"

3. Allow everyone five-to-ten minutes to arrange the eleven priorities from highest to lowest the best they can *without discussion.* Have each person keep only their top three and bottom three cards, discarding the middle five. Turn the remaining cards face down in front of each person.

4. Beginning with a layperson, work in one direction, having each person turn over their first-choice card and state a brief reason for that priority. Continue around the table until it returns to the pastor or candidate, then have him or her do the same. Allow a brief time for discussion.

5. Repeat the process with the second-choice card, then the third, and finally (if time permits) with the lowest priorities (starting with the last).

6. What do the similarities and differences suggest? What is the trend or overall picture that is seen forming? In looking at the discard pile (five middle cards), what sort of consensus is found there?

7. At the end of the game (or at the end of the meeting), ask what people feel they have learned (about themselves, about their neighbors, about their church, about their pastor/candidate). Use an easel pad or chalkboard to list the learnings. Ask if the exercise has been helpful. Enjoy it.

8

Choosing the Small Church Pastor: The Interview[1]

"For the last twenty-five years we have carried around with us the model of *manager* as cop, referee, devil's advocate, dispassionate analyst, professional, decision maker, naysayer, pronouncer. The alternative we now propose is *leader* (not manager) as cheerleader, enthusiast, nurturer of champions, hero finder, wanderer, dramatist, coach, facilitator, builder."[2]

That's a composite description Tom Peters and Nancy Austin came up with after their analyses of the leaders of America's best-run (not necessarily biggest) companies. In their book, *A Passion for Excellence: The Leadership Difference*, they point out many qualities, actions, and concepts shared by the very best transformational leaders. Not surprisingly many of the qualities, actions, and concepts are also common among the best transformational small church pastors. After all, doesn't GOLDEN TRASHBAG AWARD go along with "cheerleader"? And it takes a genuine "enthusiast" to preach "Let's Thank God . . . for the Turkeys We've Been Given." Certainly "nurturer of champions" and "hero finder" bring to mind Amazing Grace and other volunteer leaders. The term "wanderer" as Peters and Austin use it refers to "Management By Wandering Around" or MBWA, and it has to do with spending less time behind a desk and more time with workers and customers *listening* to their needs and ideas.[3] Isn't that what a transformational leader (a good small church pastor) does—gets out among the people to listen to their needs and ideas? "Leading (more so than managing) is a hands-on art."[4]

Many of the chapters in this book have sought to provide various perspectives of the small church pastor regarding the elements of leadership. But because of the intense relational nature of the small church, *the leadership is heavily dependent upon personal compatibility.* Carl Dudley, in his book *Making the Small Church Effective,* declares: "The small church wants a lover."[5] They want "someone whom they feel they can know personally . . . the most frequent personal frustration for the laity is the feeling that the pastor, hiding behind that professional polish, is not a real person. They want to know the person; that is their first priority."[6]

But despite a strong gut feeling that they want a person first and a professional second, I've found that Pastor/Parish Relations Committees (PPRCs) and search committees are at a loss when interviewing prospective candidates for a pastorate. In larger churches the process is at times more like the world of business and finance—sorting resumes, looking for publishing credits, speaking engagements, civic involvement, past pay scale, education and experience—evaluating skills and qualifications. The candidate is dissected and analyzed—as if the component parts add up to the whole person. If found to be Grade A Prime, he or she is hired.

Small church search committees should interview small church pastors as persons first and as professionals second. Generally speaking, most of the candidates will possess the basic credentials in education and fitness. If the denominations have already done much of the accrediting and presorting, why not get down to pleasure?

Why not? Because most small church search committees aren't equipped with the right questions. They use large church questions, professional questions—not *person* questions! This is not the way to interview for a person to fit into the community!

Typical questions and comments I've heard at interviews include "What do you think about Christian education?" "We need new blood in the youth group, so could you tell us your plan for transfusing it?" "You'd be willing to visit, of course." "Hope your preaching is simple, because we're just simple folk here."

Sunday church school, youth group, visitation, preaching—these traditionally have been key questions at a candidate's interview. But the questions are ambiguous! They operate on several levels—one that fits the professional questions, and one that (though disguised) fits the personal questions. The "minister," a candidate who is program-oriented or task-oriented, will outline plans and programs for each answer. Based on such loaded questions, he or she will get through the interview with flying colors—but with no *inner view*—and the committee will think they're hiring a lover for a pastor.

But what the questions really mean at the *person* level are this: "Will you be active on a personal level with our kids and support our lonely Sunday church school teachers in the Christian education program?"

"Our youth are important to us. Can you be their friend and be an intimate role model for them, and not just a distant professional advisor?"

"Would you be willing to visit, not as a chore, but so we all can get to know you one-to-one, and so we can see if we want you to marry us and ours, and baptize us and ours, and bury us and ours?"

"Hope your preaching relates to us in our daily lives with our joys and problems, not with high-falutin' rhetoric and ivory-tower theology."

Small church committees need to force themselves to follow their instincts, to ask more person-oriented questions. Pretend to be interviewing for a grandmother, a person who must possess more than a degree and some skills. How about a sense of humor? A good lap to sit on and a good shoulder to cry on? Relates well to kids? (That's different than having the ability to organize and manage a group of children.) Tell good stories? Express affection well orally, in writing, by touch and attitude? Will people seriously listen to this person or will they ignore him or her? Pretend to shop for a grandmother. It's that personal and that serious.

A healthy tactic for interviewing is to ask questions that deal with possible relationships to persons in the parish.

"What would you do if a seven-year-old girl asked you to do a funeral for her pet hamster so it could go to heaven?" That was one of the best questions I ever had put to me by a PPRC. I said I would do it. In the discussion that followed they asked me why, so I explained that my personal theology told me to put people's needs before doctrine or rules. I told them that was the way I understood Jesus to have pastored. And I also said it would give the child a chance to learn and talk about death before it came to the death of a close friend or relative. The answer might not have been the one that got me the job, but it revealed much about me as a person.

Another excellent question was "What about Christmas carols during Advent?" The question seemed incomplete, so I asked them to clarify it. A man said, "Some of the carols we sing at Christmas really should be sung after Christmas Day and the birth of Jesus, but many of us like singing them in Advent."

I answered, "Why not? Even if it is theologically arguable, and even if some pastors don't allow it, if it's a tradition here, or if it's part of your town's or church's way of 'getting into the spirit,' let's do it again. And if there is confusion about it, let's bring it before the church council for discussion and clarification. Whose church is it anyway?"

Just a sidelight about the Christmas issue—I found out later that a previous pastor had "checked out okay in the PPRC interview" (answering all the *professional* questions by outlining strategies and programs), but the person later proved to be inflexible and strong-willed ("naked power wielding") regarding worship. It took between six months and a year to discover the mismatch, but by then the church was headed for a split. Better and more person-oriented interviewing could have helped that small church avert that disastrous year. The pastor, by the way, eventually moved to a larger church and has been doing a fine job in a "bigger pulpit" where professional skills are valued differently.

Besides lack of experience, there seem to be other reasons PPRCs and search committee members ask professional rather than personal questions. Many believe they are expected to ask professional questions because it is an interview with a professional. Oftentimes conference ministers, district superintendents, and other denominational officials direct the flow of questions during the interview. They naturally lean toward the professional aspects. Though usually unintentional, their presence at a meeting can intimidate small church committees into feeling that their "simple" and "personal" questions are insignificant or irrelevant. Too often (more so in appointment or episcopal systems like Methodism) the district superintendent is seen as the parent setting up a betrothal. The pastor and the parish who are soon to be wed feel that they have little to say about their marriage. (My wife, daughter, and I were once introduced as "the pastoral family" before we had a chance to fully discuss things. There were too many factors that mitigated against the match, so we acted responsibly for us and the parish, refusing the appointment.) If the match doesn't look like a good fit, someone needs to speak up responsibly. But many small churches aren't even aware of that responsibility or that option to balk. And unfortunately, many small churches are afraid they won't get as good a candidate on the second go-round. So they settle rather than select.

Though I can't suggest all the proper questions to ask in order to find a person-pastor, I can offer seven basic guidelines to help in choosing a small church pastor.

First, *take more time.* Don't get rushed into choosing on the first interview. *With the candidate's permission* (and only if it will not be letting the cat out of the bag in the pastor's present parish), make a couple of phone calls to key people in the previous pastorate (or maybe the one before that). Keep in mind to ask relational questions and not just professional ones. Pretend you're hiring a grandmother.

Second, *make the setting a person-revealing setting.* Jesus invited himself to dinner at Zacchaeus' house so he could meet Zacchaeus as a person; he didn't stay and chat with him at his tax collector's booth where he'd have ended up interviewing the professional side of Zacchaeus.

Third, *ask person questions.* Your committee is looking for a person to fit into your community and town. The person you select should also be someone who can *inspire* people, not just manage them. He or she probably should have some understanding of small town, small church, and small community values. "The Masons, the Grange, and the Rotary will probably each ask you to join. What'll you do then?" "Each year one of the three pastors in town is asked to say the prayer at the town monument on Memorial Day. How do you feel about that?"

The person you select also should be patient, ready to smile, enjoy the socializing, and appreciate the fact that "our annual meeting is two hours of small talk, chit-chat, and outright gossip followed by five minutes in which we vote to do it all the same way we did it last year!" Small church pastors have to be patient.

Fourth, *have a list of questions prepared.* The Christmas carol and pet funeral questions are good ones, but there are many others that can come from your church's collective experience and/or imagination. Though it isn't fair to match up a candidate's answers against "good old Rev. Maxwell" (who is now bigger than life), you can use a candidate's answers to build a pretty fair personality profile. Bringing up things that bugged you about the last pastor or the one before can be helpful if formed into good person-revealing questions.

Fifth, *have your church library stock a few books about the small church, and share them among the committee members.* Don't rely on only the PPRC chairperson to ask all the questions or to be the only one well advised on your needs. Share the responsibility and the training. By reading books and articles, you begin to see the uniqueness of the small church and the small church pastor. You'll also be more aware of the possibilities of your small church. Much of the reading is fun as well as instructional.

Sixth, *get beyond formalities to what is near and dear to your church and to the person who will become the next pastor.* This may be during the afternoon half of an all-day interview that includes lunch together. Or it may be at a second interview. Play The Card Game (page 95) or find some other way to get down to what's foremost on everyone's mind.

Seventh, *don't be afraid to say no or "this doesn't feel quite comfortable."* Airing the reasons may clarify some issues for everyone involved. Avoiding a mismatch may be a service to the candidate, the district superintendent or conference minister, and to your church.

Enjoy your search for a lover as your small church pastor. Don't make interviewing and hiring a chore. Look for a person, and enjoy your work.

9

For Better, for Worse: Information that Helps Candidates Decide[1]

Pastoral candidates' minds are full of questions about the small churches that advertise vacancies. Often a good candidate is considering two or more parishes but is searching for more information to help in making a decision. If information is sketchy, the decision between Handshake Community Church and Warm Smile Community Church simply may be a matter of tossing a coin. Candidates need information.

The information needed by candidates is of two types. The first type is *figures and data:* money, membership, and contractual matters. Most churches are fairly clear on these. The second type of information includes *subjective data* and *sensory stimuli.* That's what enlivens a church and community and entices a candidate. Objective data (facts and figures) don't describe an exciting small church any more than a bunch of feathers describe a live bird (it could be a pillow). Candidates really need both types of information to make a decision.

Small churches easily can put together a variety of information that will present an honest profile of themselves. The size of the church will dictate just how much of the following information is necessary. Mid-size churches will want to include more than small churches, and the availability of both data and data gatherers will at times be a limiter. Some of the information needn't be provided unless a candidate requests it. The point is: *for both the candidate and the church, adequate information can facilitate a clear turndown or an enthusiastic acceptance.*

Congregational Statistics

If the statistics are accurate they can help the candidate to see an overall picture of the church in terms of its people and its finances. The membership secretary, treasurer, or board of deacons can provide this information fairly easily.

1. What is the recorded membership for each of the past five years? Spotting a trend might help in planning for the future.

2. What has been the average worship attendance for each of the past five years? Large membership rolls do not necessarily reflect participation, but worship figures give a more accurate picture of the activity of members.

3. What is the age distribution of members? The United Church of Christ profile sheets use a breakdown by age groupings within a decade (for example, under ten, ten to twenty, twenty to thirty, and so forth). In addition to age breakdowns, a look at family types is helpful (single, divorced, married, widowed, single parent, and so forth). A pastor may excel in ministries for single adults and see a place his or her skills can be well used; or the data may be helpful in planning an outreach program for single parents who need day care. Sex distribution might also be helpful.

4. What is the breakdown by employment types? This will help a pastor know if he or she will feel in culture. (Having been raised on a farm and having served as a Farm Bureau insurance agent made me a better match for several of the rural farming communities in which I've served.) Employment data (or unemployment data) can provide some insights into the financial base of the community. A suburban small church made up of IBM executives or middle

managers will differ from a rural small church where the steel or textile mills have died out. Another factor to weigh is the education levels of congregation members (what percentage high school graduates, or had *some* college, college grads, and so forth).

5. Treasurer's reports for past five years in addition to the current budget. Are there trends? Is there stability? (Read Chapter 7 regarding the financial support needed to maintain a church with a full-time pastor nowadays compared to thirty years ago.) If a church has just made the jump from part-time to full-time pastor, is the financial base sufficient to support the change this year? next year after a pay raise? in five years?

6. How is the budget financed? This question requires information concerning endowments and cash reserves if they are used in support of the church's budget. How about indebtedness and its repayment schedule? Does the church use a pledging system? What are the major fund-raisers? How do people feel about them? How much of the budget depends on gifts and outside donations? (In some Maine logging communities or "company towns," the paper companies will donate an amount like $10,000 to the local schools and local churches annually.) How reliable are those outside gifts from local businesses and individuals?

7. What is the distribution of member giving? This information should suggest relative stability and seek to determine if the giving is from a broad base or predominately from a select few. (Leading to issues of control later.)

8. What amount of giving goes to benevolence support? This may indicate the mission consciousness of the church.

Organizational and Administrative Data

1. A current copy of the constitution and bylaws, when analyzed, can provide a concise picture of the organization of the church and how it operates (at least in theory). When is the last time the bylaws were revised? The date of the

revision may suggest how seriously a church takes its bylaws and constitution.

2. Is there an organizational manual or a set of policy statements regarding church functions (for example, wedding charges, funeral procedure, building use, and rental instructions)? Are there any leases describing property owned by the church but rented to other organizations such as Head Start, Alcoholics Anonymous, Parents Without Partners, and so on? These are important for financial data, but they also reveal what nonprofit organizations the church supports as worthwhile ministries. The organization manual will give an idea how formally the administration of the church is carried out.

3. A current roster (with names) of the boards and committees of the church will help in assessing the power and accountability structures. When the same name starts to appear on many different boards, an important person has been spotted.

4. What organizations (formal and informal) operate within the life of the church? Such groups provide entry points into the church and can be expanded later.

History of the Congregation

1. Many churches will have a history of their church. Either someone has unofficially kept one or there has been a history compiled for a centennial or other anniversary. A sense of the church's role in the development of the community can be learned from the history. It will also be a valuable tool for determining how the church is viewed by the community.

2. How long did the last five pastors serve? When revealed, this information (for better or for worse) gives an indication of how cooperative the congregation will be with their new pastor. It may also tip a pastor off to the fact that the previous pastors and the congregation have been unsuccessful (or unaware) in dealing with the social change that has the ground shifting under their feet. (See Chapter 7

about Rockminster and Bloomberg.) Another unpleasant fact of life: it is very hard for a congregation to make a transition to a new pastor if the last one was a long-term one and was well loved. The new person on the block may find he or she is an unwitting interim who is merely a stopgap person until the next long-term pastor comes along. Finding the median age of the last five pastors will uncover a trend (if one exists) of the age preference the congregation has for its pastors.

3. What is the date of construction of the present church building? From this it is possible to gain insight into the cost of maintaining the physical plant. By installing a new oil-fired system in the main building and another in the parsonage, one Vermont church saved almost $5,000 per year. The cost of installing both units was less than $8,000, so it paid for itself in less than two years. Furthermore, the savings per year more than covered the pastor's salary and benefit increases, allowing that small church to keep him much longer than the original financial data would have suggested. Ask the board of trustees for information.

4. What is the capacity of the sanctuary and the Christian education facilities? If church growth is seriously anticipated and worked for, there must be room to grow or money for expansion. Ask the board of trustees for information.

Community Profile

1. What is the population of the surrounding community? Is it a declining or growing area? Is it inner city, suburban, rural, small town, crossroads? Are there a high number of transients? Ask at town offices, police stations.

2. How many churches are in the same area, and what denominations do they represent? An abundance of fundamental or conservative churches might wave a red flag to a liberal pastor (or it might serve to throw down the gauntlet). It would certainly suggest something about the makeup of the area. This data also provides a ratio of churches to popu-

lation. Population shifts have often left an area overloaded with churches all trying to stay afloat. Federated and union churches (especially in rural New England) have developed as a result, and pastoring a dual congregation can require special skills.

3. What is the area's economic base? Oil as in Texas? Defunct textile mills or dying tool shops in Vermont and New Hampshire (Rockminster and Bloomberg in Chapter 6)? Steel mills in Pennsylvania? Auto plants in Michigan?

4. Do any community organizations use the church facilities? A pastor may soon be at odds with his or her board of trustees if the church's general policy has not been favorable to Alcoholics Anonymous groups, community soup kitchens, and so forth, but he or she has strong feelings that the church's ministry ought to be in that direction.

5. To what extent is the pastor involved in community activities? Is there an unspoken expectation that every pastor at Pickett's Corners Church will join the Masonic Lodge? How about preaching the baccalaureate service for the high school graduation or offering the benediction for the Grange Hall's "Citizen of the Year" award night? How about school board and small town politics? Perhaps the church doesn't want the pastor to engage in any activities outside the church.

6. What communication is there between the church and community? Newsletters? Radio? Television? The communications a church uses will affect its visibility in the community. If there is no recognition of the church by the community, there will be little growth.

Church Life and Ministry

1. Rank the following from one to seven in order of their importance as pastoral tasks. (One is top priority.)

    Administration
    Visitation of the sick and aged
    General visitation to present members

Visitation to potential members
Counseling
Preaching and worship leadership
Teaching (adults and some involvement in church school)

This is best done by a church's governing board or during a supervised planning session. Sending it out in a newsletter with a return address seems fine, but it produces distorted results. This variation on The Card Game (page 95) will be a fair indicator whether the church and candidate are even negotiating within the same universe. Regardless of the validity of these rankings, this scale does provide a picture of how members view their own situation.

2. Is the church worship service formal, informal, or varied? Here is a chance to avoid mismatching a "high church" minister with a "low church" congregation (and vice versa). A pastor with high regard for the drama and beauty of traditional worship probably would not have introduced a new metaphor for baptism like "the kiss of Jesus on the forehead" (Chapter 1). And there probably would not have been all those people up at the altar for the baptism, nor would the children have been sticking their fingers in the water! It is also good to talk about lay participation in worship here. (This information may not be conveyed *before* an interview, but it is important *during* an interview.)

3. How open are members to changes within the life of the church? (open) 1 2 3 4 5 (closed). This survey might be taken at a board meeting or a planning retreat, the figures charted and averaged. Given some inevitable differences between the candidate's style and the church's "normal" way of doing things, how much room is there for compromise?

4. How does the church view ministry—as pastor only, pastor and deacons, or pastor and the laity? Failure to understand the congregation's viewpoint can lead to many misunderstandings and to much frustration.

5. How does the congregation view pastoral leadership? The pastor as lone ranger with all the authority? As a resource person enabling lay discussions of faith questions? As an answer-giver, naysayer, manager? Or as a cheerleader, coach, and leader among many leaders?

6. How involved is the church in denominational activities? Not only does this say something about the church's view of itself in relation to the church universal, but if a church is uninvolved and has a pastor who is very involved, there will be jealous feelings later regarding pastoral time.

7. How much emphasis is there on social concerns? The answer here will reveal something of how the church sees the larger church's role in the world. It will also point up early any chasm between pastor and parish in this area.

8. How do you rate the church's strengths and weaknesses? (strong) 1 2 3 4 5 (weak). Poll the church board and list results.

> Sunday worship
> Christian education
> Youth activities
> Administration (effective organization)
> Lay leadership
> Ministry to shut-ins
> Young adult ministry (singles and families)
> Community outreach
> Fellowship events together

This helps match the skills and tools of the pastor to the church, and may uncover some needs on the part of members to bolster certain areas.

Programming

1. List the current programs. Which are considered essential and important? Which are not?

2. Which current programs have been going for ten years or more? Three years or less? These will reveal which pro-

grams have achieved "traditional" status and won't be subjected to substantial changes.

3. Which program is most rewarding and effective? This will focus the strengths of the church's ministry.

4. What sort of Christian education program exists in the church? Obtain statistics of attendance and age distribution. Is teacher turnover related to the curriculum? Is there an adult component to Christian education? (If not, the real message the Christian education program broadcasts to the children may be: "Christian education is for kids, but if you put up with it, you can be free of it as adults." Does the church provide intergenerational events for Christian education?

5. To what degree are laity involved in program development? (almost always) 1 2 3 4 5 (almost never). The key here is to understand how much of the responsibility is to be placed on the pastor and how much is shared program development with the laity. High lay input usually means high "ownership" and involvement.

6. What percentage of those who attend worship will attend special programs? This seeks to find how strong the congregational support is for programming.

7. Is there or has there been a lay visitation program? This is to ascertain the church's response to the concept of shared ministry. There is often a great difference in perception between pastor and people.

Clergy Compensation and Related Considerations

1. What is included in the financial package for the pastor? The following are generally included in a complete compensation package: cash base, parsonage or housing allowance, utilities, car allowance, health insurance (often includes family coverage), pension/annuity, continuing education, vacation, and days off. Some packages also include a provision for a sabbatical leave and/or a specified amount of money for social security offset.

2. Specific details about the parsonage should be in writing. Questions of maintenance, snow and trash removal, and lawn mowing need to be dealt with early so misunderstandings won't cause hard feelings later. Planned improvements should be stated and asked about.

Provisions for the pastor's leisure needs should be made. A congregation in New Hampshire had bought a new modular home and placed it behind the church on a lot only slightly larger than the home itself. There was no shrubbery around the house at all, and the whole busy downtown could look right through a vacant lot into the parsonage. When the pastor brought the issue up, the congregation thought he was complaining about a lack of privacy and wanted a hedge to block the view. But the issue wasn't privacy. It was that there wasn't any sort of yard for leisure activity. The pastor felt like a prisoner in his own parsonage, a parsonage that was built with only the business side of the pastor in mind, not the whole person. (They are now talking about building a deck on the off-street side, and installing a sliding door to get to it without parading out the front door for all the town to see.

3. How many marriages and funerals are performed (on average) annually for nonmembers? Is this excellent form of evangelism looked on favorably by the church? What is the average honorarium for a funeral or wedding of a nonchurch member? This will increase the pastor's income a bit. Ask the local funeral director for this information.

4. How will the congregation react if the pastor takes two days a week off? Personal and family time are essential, especially if the pastor is to continue to function effectively for a long-term pastorate. The parish needs to protect good pastors.

5. How many hours is a pastor expected to work to be considered full-time?

6. Is there a study or is the pastor expected to work out of his or her home? Often families in the parsonage make it difficult (not intentionally) for a good counseling session

to take place if the office is in the home. Also related is the question of the church phone number being the same as the parsonage phone.

7. If the parsonage is close to the church, is the pastor expected to serve as caretaker for the church and/or church grounds? How will this affect the relational caring time the pastor is expected to spend in the parish?

8. Is there a provision for cost-of-living increases in the pastor's financial package? The more that is planned in advance for cost-of-living and merit raises, the easier it will be to deal with in the future. Paying a good small church pastor is difficult these days.

9. How would the congregation react if the pastor wanted to supplement his or her income during time off, such as teaching an evening course, giving flying lessons, or doing freelance photography?

10. Is there a regular evaluation of pastoral services? Many problems can be avoided before they cause explosions. The Card Game helps, but appraisals are also excellent.

11. How does the church view the pastor's spouse? One needs to be clear about hidden expectations on spouses. Hiring two-for-one is no longer acceptable.

Subjective Data and Sensory Stimuli (or Do you love to dance the cha-cha? items)

1. What about hospitals and schools, doctors, dentists, gymnastics classes for the teenage daughter? Is there a YMCA or YWCA with a running track? How about a community swimming pool? If my interest is in basketball, is there a town or area men's league? colleges? What about canoeing? Backpacking, hiking, fishing, hunting? Where are the nearest state parks and national forests? Is there a historic city like Boston or San Antonio nearby? a preschool program? bowling alleys and leagues? golf courses? a small municipal airport for the pastor-pilot? The candidate may ask for information on these based on questions he or she

and the family may come up with. Or the church may readily supply such information.

2. My spouse is a pickle boat captain. What about nearby employment for him or her?

3. My son is in a wheelchair (or has special needs). Are the church and parsonage accessible (or will they be)? Why or why not?

4. My family and I like to hike the Appalachian Trail (or we bike across America every summer). As a way for us to do that, and as a way for the church to save $600 in its budget, I'd like to take an additional two weeks off in the summer without pay. It's a slack time, and we have lay leadership who would love to preach. What about that idea? Can we negotiate?

5. We haven't got a dog now, but we thought our kids ought to grow up with one as we did. Or maybe a pony. Is there room? Are there objections?

6. Smoking? Drinking? How about pastors and/or spouses being seen in their yard/garden in shorts? Halter tops?

7. Is there room for a garden to be planted? Will some of you help us plant it? If we aren't arriving until mid-July, would a few of you plant it for us this first year?

8. What are the main leisure activities in the community?

A pastor friend had to choose between two small churches in Kansas after he and his spouse decided they wanted to leave New England to return and raise their children in the Midwest as they themselves had been raised. The two churches were about even on paper and after the interview, but he chose not to go to the one whose town was known primarily for its stock car race track. He not only didn't enjoy it, but it also created a negative image for him. The *feel* of stock car racing permeated the town. He didn't want that for his family.

9. Are there clergy specials? Many clergy refuse discounts in stores, but some accept preferential treatment under certain conditions (services but not goods). Several Vermont

golf courses, recognizing the low salaries and high leisure/ getaway needs of Vermont and New Hampshire clergypersons, offer free golf.

A special drawing card in the area I now serve is free college courses at Dartmouth College (a longstanding tradition). At more than $1,000 per course, and with their fine religion department, that's nothing to sneeze at!

There are dozens of questions candidates and their families are dying to ask about the community they'll be joining as well as the church the clergyperson will be serving. And there are dozens of "fringe benefits" that churches can brag about before or during the interview. By dividing up the data-gathering tasks, and by not meeting more than is necessary (until sufficient data is collected to produce a healthy section of a profile), a small church can begin to differentiate itself from another church that looks the same in statistics. As the church works harder and harder to present a clear picture of who it is to the candidate, the chances of attracting and keeping a good small church pastor increase thirty, sixty, even a hundredfold.

Conclusion

Until three years ago two small churches in Vermont had shared a part-time pastor. But after a half-dozen years there, the pastor decided that he felt torn, as if he was serving two masters. With an eight-to-five job in addition to the parishes, his was an exhausting life. His heart was more invested in one church than in the other, something not uncommon in such "yoked" situations. He had developed a deep pastoral love relationship with one church and he wanted to spend even more time with them.

The situation changed and the yoke was broken because another part-time pastor (also with an eight-to-five job) became available in that geographic area. The administrative separation occurred and each church jumped at the chance to have their own pastor.

Before the "unyoking" the worship attendances were fifteen and ten in the two churches (respectively). The new pastor assumed duties at the smaller church and the old pastor continued at the larger church.

Now, three years later, *attendance is unchanged but both churches are thriving.* There has been no numerical growth. The differences are: there is now a Sunday church school of four children in the church that had had none; each church now has a monthly fellowship supper followed by a laity-led

Bible study (where previously there were no Bible studies); financial giving is up (slightly); both churches have begun investing tremendous amounts of personal energies in cleaning their churchyards and sprucing up their buildings inside and out; the people feel good about themselves individually and corporately.

What has made the difference? What has been the catalyst? I'm sure the Holy Spirit has been active, but it's also largely due to the change in the leadership dynamics.

Both churches now have pastors who are lovers. But the greatest transformation has occurred in the smaller church. (The larger church had begun to be transformed during the six years its current pastor had been there.) The smaller church never truly felt loved or esteemed. Instead it always felt inadequate and unloved, describing itself as "the poorer cousin" to the church with five more people at worship.

Now each church has a pastor who "attends," who really *listens to* and *feels* the needs of the Body, and helps them discover the resources they have (and the resources they are) to take care of the needs. Lay leadership is springing forth like spring crocuses, and people are filling roles. There is a renewed sense of esteem, identity, and purpose for each church (but especially for the smaller one). The difference, I believe, is the pastoral lover, and a *leadership that is relational.*

The effect is not growth in numbers—but growth in the sense that "we are a church." More people are actively volunteering; there is a visible appreciation system; there is a sense of mission beyond ourselves; there is a *realistic* outlook toward ministry tasks, the focus having shifted from what we *can't* do to what we *can* do. And the creative ideas are bursting forth.

The smaller church did not have much of a selection when it came to securing a pastor, but they had a choice. They did not have to say yes, and they either could have stayed where they were or looked elsewhere. But they chose a pastor they thought would love them. They chose a pastor who felt like a person first, who was real and down to earth. They chose a pastor who was a relational leader, a small church pastor.

And because of their choice, they are now a well-functioning, healthy, vibrant small church.

They, and thousands of small churches like them, are what this book is all about. May God bless them and their leaders, both laity and clergy.

Selected Annotated Bibliography

Brown, Carolyn C. *Developing Christian Education in the Smaller Church.* Nashville: Abingdon Press, 1982. The sections on finding and training teachers and what to expect from the small church pastor are very insightful.

Burns, James MacGregor. *Leadership.* New York: Harper and Row, Publishers Inc., 1978. Burns's Pulitzer-prize-winning book redefines leadership in a revolutionary way.

Burt, Steven E. "Planning Retreat: Taking the Pulse of Your Church," *Your Church,* January/February 1983, p. 33 ff. Discusses planning sessions for small churches.

————————. "Choosing the Small Church Pastor," *Your Church,* September/October 1984, p. 42 ff. Urges selection of pastors for small churches on a person-before-professional basis. Hints for lay leaders in the interview process.

————————. "How to Write Litanies," *Your Church,* November/December 1984, p. 22 ff. An article developed around the idea of the intimacy of small churches in their corporate worship experience.

————————. "Our Church Cares (Ten Ways to Show It)," *Your Church,* September/October 1985, p. 14 ff. A communications article suggesting that small churches allow their ministries to be defined by perceived needs, and that the ministries need to project a clear image of the local church.

_____. "Ten Good Reasons for Church Suppers," *Your Church*, May/June 1986. Urges evaluation of small church programs and ministry not on a one-point basis, but by considering the impact from a variety of angles.

_____. "True Worship," *The Upper Room*, July 23, 1983. The true story of the solidarity of a small Maine congregation that halted its Sunday worship in mid-service to gather food, clothing, and money, which they delivered to a family whose home was destroyed by fire the night before.

Carroll, Jackson W., ed. *Small Churches Are Beautiful.* San Francisco: Harper and Row, Publishers Inc., 1977. The product of a Hartford Seminary colloquium on small churches, this book was the first in the small church movement. It is valuable not only for itself, but also because it identifies several authors who contributed significantly to the field of the small church.

Cook, Walter L. *Send Us a Minister . . . Any Minister Will Do*. Rockland, Maine: Courier-Gazette, 1978. The author of this insightful book, Walter Cook, was a field education director and professor of Pastoral Care at Bangor Seminary.

Crandall, Ronald K., and Sells, L. Ray. *There's New Life in the Small Congregation! Why It Happens and How.* Nashville: Discipleship Resources, 1983. Although it rehashes much of the current popular material from Dudley, Schaller, Walrath, and the Hartford Seminary Foundation, it is valuable for its several case studies and for the data compiled from a small membership church survey.

Dudley, Carl S. *Unique Dynamics of the Small Church.* Washington: The Alban Institute, 1977. A slim but important booklet that focuses on the "single cell" nature of the small church.

_____. *Making the Small Church Effective.* Nashville: Abingdon Press, 1978. The most influential book about small church yet published. Much observation of small church interaction and intimacy. Focus on the pastor as lover and generalist, plus comparison of small church's behavior to extended family.

_____. *Where Have All Our People Gone?* New York: The Pilgrim Press, 1979. A book that prompts congregations to wake up and look at the social change that has occurred around them. A look at the baby boom years of the 1950s and 1960s. What it means to churches trying to "keep up with the 1958 Jones's."

Dunkin, Steve. *Church Advertising: A Practical Guide.* Nashville: Abingdon Press, 1982. From the Abingdon Creative Leadership Series, edited by Lyle Schaller. Dunkin's book is more applicable to larger churches, but the section about advertising strategy ("Describe Your Target (Exactly!)") is helpful when its concept is used to design ministry strategies small churches can use to meet needs and attract potential members.

Fowler, James W. *Stages of Faith: The Psychology of Human Development and the Quest for Meaning.* San Francisco: Harper and Row, Publishers Inc., 1981. Important in helping leaders to understand the transition events in life and how the small church plays a part in them.

Friedman, Edwin H. *Generation to Generation: Family Process in Church and Synagogue.* New York: The Guilford Press, 1985. Although Rabbi Friedman's book is a theory text for family therapy practitioners, the observations, ideas, and prescriptions are wonderful helps for those wanting to understand the small church.

Gallup, George, Jr. *Religion in America 1984.* Princeton: The Princeton Religion Research Center, Inc., March 1984. Trends and attitudes of Americans compared with past Gallup polls. Offers substantive data that may help small churches redirect some of their energies. Can also help dispel some common misconceptions that lead to blaming failure of the organization on the leadership.

Glasse, James D. *Putting It Together in the Parish.* Nashville: Abingdon Press, 1972. The fourth chapter, "Living in the Maintenance/Mission Bind," is helpful, particularly the section dealing with pastors "paying the rent."

Hoge, Dean R. and Roozen, David A., eds. *Understanding Church Growth and Decline 1950–1978.* New York: The Pilgrim Press, 1979. It is crucial that leaders in small churches understand the decline of the church so they can conceptualize and strategize for growth. A particularly relevant chapter is Douglas Walrath's chapter on "Social Change and Local Churches: 1951–1975."

Johnson, Douglas W. *The Care and Feeding of Volunteers.* Nashville: Abingdon Press, 1978. Part of the Abingdon Creative Leadership Series, edited by Lyle Schaller. Some important ideas about appreciation and acknowledgment.

Jones, Landon Y. *Great Expectations: America and the Baby Boom Generation.* New York: Ballantine Books, 1981. Provides important understandings of the social change that resulted from the baby boom years, including church expectations that have contributed to a sense of failure in today's church (not keeping up with the way it used to be when we had three services every Sunday with sixty kids in the junior choir). This also can provide important insights into what motivates the baby boom generation that is returning to church in the 1980s and 1990s.

Kemper, Robert G. *Beginning a New Pastorate.* Nashville: Abingdon Press, 1978. Part of the Abingdon Creative Leadership Series, edited by Lyle Schaller. A heap of good advice about the selection and decision-making process pastors go through when deciding on a move. Some important ideas on the interview, including saying no.

Mathieson, Moira B. *The Shepherds of the Delectable Mountains: The Story of the Washington County Mission Program.* Cincinnati: Foreward Movement Publications, 1979. A well-documented mission experiment in rural Maryland. It is important because it involved small churches and relied heavily on laypersons who were trained to perform what are typically thought of as clergy functions. Resolution of conflict and a development of trust in a working clergy/ lay relationship provide useful information.

Morse, H. N. and Brunner, Edmund. *The Town and Country Church in the United States.* New York: George H. Doran Company, 1923. Provides some interesting statistics and data about small churches in small communities. It is helpful in seeing the number of families or pledging units that used to be needed to support a full-time pastor (compared to today). It can help one to understand why pastors today are stressed out.

Naisbitt, John. *Megatrends: Ten New Directions Transforming Our Lives.* New York: Warner Books, 1984. The implications of several of the trends the author describes are important for small churches. If adults are inclined to improving themselves physically, spiritually, and emotionally (a shift from focusing all their energies onto their children as the 1950s parents did), the church needs to look at adult education rather than junior church school. At the very least it needs to change the program priorities if it is to meet the needs today.

Oswald, Roy M. *New Beginnings: Pastoral Start Up Workbook.* Washington: The Alban Institute, 1977. The book is worth it just for the section on termination and the emotions around it—for the pastor, family, and the church family. With the small church, since the pastor is experienced as person first and professional second, the emotion is likely to be more intense than in a large church.

Peters, Thomas J. and Waterman, Robert H., Jr. *In Search of Excellence: Lessons from America's Best-run Companies.* New York: Warner Books, 1984. Some important distinctions between management and leadership offered. Some of the important elements of successful business include responding to customer needs, taking the customer seriously, and listening to the production people. Much of this easily translates to better ways churches need to "take care of business" (meeting ministry needs).

Peters, Tom and Austin, Nancy. *A Passion for Excellence: The Leadership Difference.* New York: Random House, 1985. An expansion of *In Search of Excellence,* this book narrows the subject to leadership. Many excellent chapters about leader's roles and functions. Especially helpful in drawing clear distinctions between leadership and management. Good section on purpose of an organization and another on motivation.

Ray, David R. *Small Churches Are the Right Size.* New York: The Pilgrim Press, 1982. Ray's book is one of the most favorable to small churches and affirms not only their uniqueness, but also their worth. The sections on mission and stewardship are very good.

Sanderson, Dwight. *Rural Sociology and Rural Social Organization.* New York: John Wiley and Sons, Inc., 1942. It would be unfair to compare the present-day small church only to the small church of the baby boom 1950s and 1960s. Two sections are noteworthy in Sanderson's book: "The Program of the Rural Church" and "Ministerial Leadership."

Schaller, Lyle E. *The Local Church Looks to the Future: A Guide to Church Planning.* Nashville: Abingdon Press, 1968. The chapter entitled "What Is Our Purpose?" is important if leaders are to work together toward a common end.

_____. *Parish Planning: How to Get Things Done in Your Church.* Nashville: Abingdon Press, 1971. Good section on purpose, expectations, and evaluation. Also important in that a chapter acknowledges that different types of congregations need to plan differently.

_____. *The Change Agent: The Strategy of Innovative Leadership.* Nashville: Abingdon Press, 1972. A genuinely helpful chapter about power and power relationships. Schaller takes power (what I would call authority) apart and analyzes it. A major discovery is that power doesn't necessarily come with the office of pastor. "The exercise of power is determined by values and relationships."

_____. *The Pastor and the People*. Nashville: Abingdon Press, 1973. One of the real gifts Schaller has given the church (and especially me). His "Card Game" of pastoral priorities is something I have reworked and use often.

_____. *Hey, That's Our Church!* Nashville: Abingdon Press, 1975. A good overview of types of churches and stages of maturity in churches. Developmental as well as geographical understanding.

_____. *Understanding Tomorrow*. Nashville: Abingdon Press, 1976. One of the best popular church books around, this book helps get a handle on the effects of social change on the American church since World War II. Schaller looks at the baby boom years, mobility, the shift from verbal to visual ways of learning, the urban exodus, and much more. By reading this, church leaders could reduce the unnecessary guilt many churches carry.

_____. *Survival Tactics in the Parish*. Nashville: Abingdon Press, 1977. Although very anecdotal in its style, there is much excellent theory relating to the small church. Chapters like "Be Sure to Thank Dorothy!" and "What Do We Look Like to You?" are valuable both for the pastor and the leaders involved in serious self-assessment. Another excellent point is made about acknowledging volunteer's efforts in the chapter entitled "Silver Beavers or Dead Rats?"

_____. *Assimilating New Members*. Nashville: Abingdon Press, 1978. Excellent points about inclusion, exclusion, group life, and the different ways churches (of different sizes) attract and assimilate members.

_____. *Activating the Passive Church: Diagnosis and Treatment*. Nashville: Abingdon Press, 1981. The points about apathy, indifference, and low self-esteem are well made. Also some good points about pastor/church mismatches that challenge the idea that pastors are simply interchangeable professional pawns.

_____. *The Small Church Is Different!* Nashville: Abingdon Press, 1982. Along with Dudley's *Making the Small Church Effective* and Ray's *Small Churches Are the Right Size,* this is the finest work available for offering insight into the workings of the small church.

_____. *Growing Plans: Strategies to Increase Your Church's Membership.* Nashville: Abingdon Press, 1983. Despite the fact that I take issue with the stated goal in Schaller's title (institutional survival is implied by a focus on membership gains rather than exposing people to the gospel), there are many important strategies outlined here—the idea being to bring people into the church (and hold them there). Only one quarter of the book relates to growth in small churches.

_____. *Looking in the Mirror: Self-Appraisal in the Local Church.* Nashville: Abingdon Press, 1984. The section on cats, collies, and ranches (different size churches) is a gem simply because it provides a fresh and helpful way of seeing varieties of pastor/church relationships as size changes. The book is also very helpful in getting churches started at basic self-appraisal and planning.

Schirer, Marshall E. and Forehand, Mary Anne. *Cooperative Ministry: Hope for Small Churches.* Valley Forge: Judson Press, 1984. Cooperative parishes are ways smaller churches can join forces to accomplish ministry goals. This is not a survival tactic or a way of gaining the services of a pastor (as are yoked parishes and federations). The goal is ministry, not minister. In that regard the book is quite helpful, but it fails to discuss the full ramifications of joint ministry (especially the negatives).

Stevenson, J. W. *God in My Unbelief.* New York: Harper and Row, Publishers Inc., 1960. Not a text, but still helpful in understanding the small parish. Stevenson's descriptions of the groups within the church and of the difficulty in introducing change are valuable.

Surrey, Peter J. *The Small Town Church.* Nashville: Abingdon Press, 1981. Part of the Abingdon Creative Leadership

Series, edited by Lyle Schaller. Written as a series of letters from an older parishioner to a young pastor, the advice is sound and helpful in understanding the dynamics of a small town and a small church.

Walrath, Douglas Alan. *Leading Churches Through Change.* Nashville: Abingdon Press, 1979. Part of the Abingdon Creative Leadership Series, edited by Lyle Schaller. Several excellent case studies including a cluster approach to small church ministry (showing good and bad) and two mergers (one successful and one unsuccessful).

_____. "Finding Options for Ministry in Small Churches: A Report to the Program Committee for Professional Church Leadership." New York: National Council of Churches, February 1981. Brief look at the distinctive characteristics, difficulties, and options for small churches.

_____, ed. *New Possibilities for Small Churches.* New York: The Pilgrim Press, 1983. Two chapters stand out in this book by small church experts— Walrath's "Possibilities for Small Churches Today," and Dudley's "The Art of Pastoring a Small Congregation." Dudley gets right to the heart of the small church with an economy of words.

Westerhoff, John H. III and Neville, Gwen Kennedy. *Generation to Generation: Conversations on Religious Education and Culture.* New York: United Church Press, 1974; reprint ed., New York: The Pilgrim Press, 1979. Important concepts and ideas having to do with religious socialization. Especially important in conjunction with Dudley's theory and observations that small churches are "culture carrying" congregations.

Westerhoff, John H. III. *Will Our Children Have Faith?* New York: Seabury Press, 1976. Solid theory about religious socialization—especially concerning the impact of intergenerational experience and modeling (especially helpful in programming the small church).

Willimon, William H. and Wilson, Robert L. *Preaching and Worship in the Small Church.* Nashville: Abingdon Press,

1980. Generally helpful in understanding small church worship, but it is too much focused from the pastor's point of view. At times it feels as if it is too theoretical, too much from a seminary idealist's perspective. Needs to be understood in tandem with Dudley's and Schaller's ideas of worship as a "folk dance."

Notes

Introduction

[1] Steve Burt, "True Worship," *The Upper Room* devotional guide, vol. 49, no. 3 (Nashville: The Upper Room, 1983), p. 28.

[2] Helen G. Taylor, "Good Mourning," *Leadership 100,* March-April 1983, p. 22.

Chapter 1

[1] For a refreshing look at the differences between large and small churches, see Carl S. Dudley, *Making the Small Church Effective* (Nashville: Abingdon Press, 1978), Chapter 1; see also David R. Ray, *Small Churches Are the Right Size* (New York: The Pilgrim Press, 1982), Chapter 2.

[2] For some fresh insights into the differences between small and large churches (but don't carry the comparison too far), see Carl S. Dudley, "Affectional and Directional Orientations to Faith," publication no. AL 60 from the Alban Institute, 4125 Nebraska Avenue NW, Washington, D.C. 20016.

[3] Lyle E. Schaller, *The Small Church Is Different* (Nashville: Abingdon Press, 1982), page 133.

[4] Burt, "True Worship" in its entirety.

[5] Dudley, *Effective,* Chapter 2: "The Caring Cell."

[6] Schaller, *Small Church,* page 135.

[7] *Ibid.,* page 30.

[8] David Ray makes several excellent points about informal Christian education in Chapter 4 of *Small Churches Are the Right Size.* For a broad overview of modeling and Christian education by observation of models, see John W. Westerhoff III, *Will Our Children Have Faith?* (New York: The Seabury Press, 1976).

[9] Schaller, *Small Church,* page 29.

[10] Carl Dudley, "The Art of Pastoring a Small Congregation," in *New Possibilities for Small Churches,* ed. Douglas Alan Walrath (New York: The Pilgrim Press, 1983), p. 47.

[11] Schaller, *Small Church,* p. 29.

[12] *Ibid.,* p. 28. Also in Ray, *Right Size,* p. 46.

[13] Douglas W. Johnson, *The Care and Feeding of Volunteers* (Nashville: Abingdon Press, 1978), Chapter 1.

[14] Schaller, *Small Church,* p. 11.
[15] Ray, *Right Size,* p. 154.
[16] Interviews with members of small church search committees and pastor-parish relations committees between 1981 and 1985.

Chapter 2

[1] Dudley, "The Art of Pastoring . . . " in *New Possibilities,* p. 57.
[2] Douglas Alan Walrath, "Possibilities for Small Churches Today," in *New Possibilities,* picking up the concept described in pp. 21–27.
[3] Dudley, *Effective,* pp. 72–73.
[4] Margery Williams, *The Velveteen Rabbit* (New York: Avon Books, 1975). (Idea suggested in Ray, *Right Size,* Chapter 6.)
[5] Schaller, *Small Church,* p. 32.
[6] Dudley, in *New Possibilities,* p. 51.
[7] Paraphrase of an anecdote used by Carl Dudley in a workshop for federated churches, given at Bristol, Vermont, during October 1983. Its essence is also found in Dudley, *Effective,* p. 130.
[8] Douglas Alan Walrath, spring 1983 lecture at Bangor Theological Seminary, Bangor, Maine.

Chapter 3

[1] Ray, *Right Size,* p. 114.
[2] The "attraction model" is discussed in Schaller's *Small Church* on pp. 39–40.
[3] Ray, *Right Size,* p. 151.
[4] James MacGregor Burns, *Leadership* (New York: Harper & Row, Publishers Inc., 1978), p. 18.
[5] *Ibid.,* p. 19.
[6] Ray, *Right Size,* p. 51.
[7] Dudley, in *New Possibilities,* p. 46.
[8] Burns, *Leadership,* p. 20.
[9] *Ibid.*
[10] For a fuller discussion of transactional leadership see Burns, *Leadership,* p. 19.
[11] Walrath, in *New Possibilities,* pp. 17–18.

Chapter 4

[1] Tom Peters and Nancy Austin, *A Passion for Excellence: The Leadership Difference* (New York: Random House, 1985), p. xix.
[2] The *Upper Room* and *Discipleship* resources catalogs are available free by writing to them at 1908 Grand Avenue, P.O. Box 189, Nashville, Tennessee 37202.
[3] Neighborhood Bible Studies, Inc., Dobbs Ferry, New York 10522.
[4] Thomas J. Peters and Robert H. Waterman, Jr., *In Search of Excellence* (New York: Warner Books, 1984), p. 226.
[5] Edwin H. Friedman, "A Family Systems Expert Talks About Congregational Leadership," an interview conducted by Celia Allison Hahn, *Alban Institute Action Information,* vol. xi, no. 3, p. 2.
[6] *Ibid.,* p. 3.
[7] *Ibid.*
[8] Cartoon in *Leadership* magazine, summer 1985, concept by Don Byers, artwork by Larry Thomas.
[9] Schaller, *Small Church,* pp. 39–40.
[10] Peters and Waterman, *In Search of Excellence,* p. 201.
[11] Johnson, *Care and Feeding,* p. 43.
[12] 1984 Gallup Poll report, "Religion in America," p. 36.

Chapter 5

[1] Johnson, *Care and Feeding,* p. 18.

[2] *Ibid.,* pp. 24–26.

[3] Abraham H. Maslow, "A Theory of Human Motivation," *Psychological Review* 50 (1943): pp. 370–396.

[4] Joel C. Hunter, "Romancing the Congregation," *Leadership,* summer 1985.

[5] Steve Burt, "Let's Thank God . . . for the Turkeys We've Been Given," *Pulpit Digest,* July-August 1984.

Chapter 6

[1] Steve Burt, "Our Church Cares (Ten Ways to Show It)," *Your Church,* September-October 1985, illustration from p. 16.

[2] *Ibid.*

[3] Excerpted from Steve Burt, "Ten Good Reasons for Church Suppers," *Your Church,* May-June 1986.

Chapter 7

[1] Based on an April 15, 1985, article by Joann Pletto in *Valley News,* P.O. Box 877, White River Junction, Vermont 05001.

[2] A number of books address the issues of the church and social change: Lyle E. Schaller, *Understanding Tomorrow* (Nashville: Abingdon Press, 1976); Carl S. Dudley, *Where Have All Our People Gone?* (New York: The Pilgrim Press, 1979); Douglas Alan Walrath, *Leading Churches Through Change* (Nashville: Abingdon Press, 1979), especially Chapter 3.

[3] 1984 Gallup Poll report, p. 90.

[4] *Ibid.*

[5] A number of helpful books are available for assessment, planning, and goal-setting: Douglas A. Walrath, *Planning for Your Church* (Philadelphia: Westminster Press, 1984); Lyle E. Schaller, *Looking in the Mirror: Self-Appraisal in the Local Church* (Nashville: Abingdon Press, 1984); Lyle E. Schaller, *Parish Planning: How to Get Things Done in Your Church* (Nashville: Abingdon Press, 1971).

[6] "The Card Game" is based on a similar tool found in Lyle E. Schaller's *The Pastor and the People* (Nashville: Abingdon Press, 1973) and a Methodist handout entitled "The Nature and Function of Pastoral Ministry," published by the Division of Ordained Ministry, Board of Higher Education and Ministry, P.O. Box 871, Nashville, Tennessee 37202.

Chapter 8

[1] Steve Burt, "Choosing the Small Church Pastor," *Your Church,* September-October 1984, p. 42. This chapter is an expansion of my article.

[2] Peters and Austin, *A Passion for Excellence,* p. 265.

[3] *Ibid.,* Chapter 2.

[4] *Ibid.,* p. 378.

[5] Dudley, *Effective,* p. 72.

[6] *Ibid.,* p. 71.

Chapter 9

[1] My thanks to the Rev. Charles Lee Stark, former Director of Admissions at Bangor Theological Seminary, and a close friend, for allowing me to draw from "Seeking a New Church: Gathering the Data for a Decision," a paper he pre-

sented at Bangor Seminary on January 4, 1983. Most of the hard statistical data gathering is based on his work, and mine picks up again at the more personal data pastors (and churches) need to know (the do-you-like-to dance-the-cha-cha stuff).

Small Church in Action Series

Money, Motivation, and Mission in the Small Church

Anthony Pappas. An on-the-job understanding of small church culture and what motivates members. Includes nine strategies for fund-raising utilizing important strengths and characteristics of small church culture; alternate ways to pay the pastors of churches that are unable to meet their denomination's standards; how to do high-impact mission on a low budget; and an irreverent (yet practical) guide to church budgets.
0-8170-1146-3

Developing Your Small Church's Potential

Carl S. Dudley, Douglas Alan Walrath. Dynamic possibilities for churches struggling to survive despite dwindling memberships. New ideas for making positive use of community transition, absorbing newcomers into the church family, reshaping the church's image, and developing programs reflecting community needs.
0-8170-1120-X

Christian Education in the Small Church

Donald L. Griggs, Judy McKay Walther. Quality programs on a tight budget is the goal of a holistic approach to education covering all ages and all church activities. Filled with new ideas for tailoring programs to community needs, designing a curriculum, selecting the resources, building relationships between education and worship, equipping leaders, and much more.
0-8170-1103-X